TH.

RULES

OF

SUCCESS

Pearson

At Pearson, we have a simple mission: to help people make more of their lives through learning.

We combine innovative learning technology with trusted content and educational expertise to provide engaging and effective learning experiences that serve people wherever and whenever they are learning.

From classroom to boardroom, our curriculum materials, digital learning tools and testing programmes help to educate millions of people worldwide – more than any other private enterprise.

Every day our work helps learning flourish, and wherever learning flourishes, so do people.

To learn more, please visit us at **www.pearson.com**

THE
RULES
OF
SUCCESS

A personal code for
taking control of your life
and realising your ambitions

RICHARD TEMPLAR

Pearson

Harlow, England • London • New York • Boston • San Francisco • Toronto • Sydney
Dubai • Singapore • Hong Kong • Tokyo • Seoul • Taipei • New Delhi
Cape Town • São Paulo • Mexico City • Madrid • Amsterdam • Munich • Paris • Milan

PEARSON EDUCATION LIMITED
KAO Two
KAO Park
Harlow CM17 9NA
United Kingdom
Tel: +44 (0)1279 623623
Web: www.pearson.com

First edition published 2025 (print and electronic)

ISBN: 978-1-292-47474-8 (print)
       978-1-292-74268-7 (ePub)

British Library Cataloguing-in-Publication Data
A catalogue record for the print edition is available from the British Library

Library of Congress Cataloging-in-Publication Data
A catalog record for the print edition is available from the Library of Congress

10 9 8 7 6 5 4 3 2 1
29 28 27 26 25

Cover design by redeyoffdesign.com

Print edition typeset in 11/13, ITC Berkeley Oldstyle Pro by Straive
Printed in the UK by Bell and Bain Ltd, Glasgow

NOTE THAT ANY PAGE CROSS REFERENCES REFER TO THE PRINT EDITION

Contents

Time 50

Emotions 80

At work 108

Decisions 144

While we work hard to present unbiased, fully accessible content, we want to hear from you about any concerns or needs with this Pearson product so that we can investigate and address them:

- Please contact us with concerns about any potential bias at https://www.pearson.com/report-bias.html.

- For accessibility-related issues, such as using assistive technology with Pearson products, alternative text requests, or accessibility documentation, email the Pearson Disability Support team at **disability.support@pearson.com**.

Introduction

We all measure success differently according to what we prioritise in life. Ask twenty people what success means to them, and you'll get twenty slightly different – sometimes very different – answers. Money, status, a big house, a happy family, leisure time . . . we have different priorities. What's more, those priorities change as we go through life. When you're young, you might see success in terms of career and money. As time goes on, family becomes more important or time to do the things you really enjoy.

Of course, for most of us success is more nuanced than that. If you became a multi-millionaire but had no friends, it's unlikely you'd consider yourself a complete success. Similarly if you're surrounded by a loving family but struggling to put food in their mouths, you wouldn't feel your life had gone entirely to plan. And some of us really don't care about the trappings of success at all. One of my closest friends lives in a camper van – actually I've had several friends in my life who have lived in similar accommodation – and he's entirely happy. He's not remotely materialistic and loves his freedom, and this is what he's always wanted, after decades of a job he didn't specially enjoy. Only the other day someone said to me 'My threshold for success is being able to go round the supermarket without checking the price of anything. Everything beyond that is a bonus'. But I know plenty of other people who would consider themselves a failure if they weren't living in a decent house they'd bought with the money they earned.

So in order to be successful, you first need to know what that success will look like. And be prepared for that goal to shift over the years. It doesn't matter a jot what anyone else thinks. If you don't care about money, or about status, or maybe about having kids, or perhaps the house – or camper van – you live in, there's no point striving towards some artificial vision of what you think success is supposed to be. That's not going to make you happy. So forget what your parents say, or what you think society expects, and identify what success would feel like for you. You're far more likely to achieve it if you know what it is.

I've written about aspects of success before, most obviously in *The Rules of Work* and *The Rules of Wealth*. Although I could argue quite strongly that all the books in this series are about success in the various different areas of life they cover, whether that's relationships, being a parent, whatever. In fact, success is very much what I'm all about. I've had several careers in my life, before becoming a full-time writer. I worked in casinos for many years, eventually ending up as a general manager, before going on to work in the corporate sector and then running my own business. All of these have given me opportunities to study people in different environments – I'm an inveterate people-watcher – and to analyse what makes them succeed or fail, flourish or struggle. While I'm not a qualified psychotherapist myself, I have friends who are, and we often compare notes about what I've observed and they have studied.

So what makes this particular set of Rules any more likely to bring you success than the others? I've watched friends and colleagues and passing acquaintances over the years, and seen which of them achieve the goals they set themselves, and which don't quite make it. Is it pure chance, or is there something they're doing, or not doing, that gives them a better chance of succeeding? Of course there will always be elements of luck – good and bad – but I've come to realise that there are ways to skew things very much in your favour.

Look, we all want life to flow smoothly. We feel we could achieve our aims far more easily if only other things didn't get in our way. If only we had a bit more time, or weren't always worrying about money, or didn't have such a huge workload, or had more confidence, or weren't always running to keep still. And those things can snowball. If you don't have enough time, for example, you struggle to keep on top of your surroundings and find yourself living surrounded by clutter. That makes it hard to keep your mind clear and wastes time you don't have whenever you need to find a thing.

Who has been most likely to succeed then, of the countless people I've observed? Overwhelmingly, it's the people who are in control of their time, their workload, their money, their emotions. The people who can get things done easily because they make good decisions without procrastinating, they manage their relationships effectively, they're productive at work, they function in an uncluttered world where there is room for them to focus on the things that matter to them, without getting bogged down in the minutiae that other people trip over.

These people control their own world, they don't let it control them. Of course they hit the occasional unanticipated crisis, as we all do, but they navigate it more effectively because they've given themselves more room for manoeuvre, more slack in the system, and they know what they're doing. On their worst days, they're doing fine. On their best days, they're gliding effortlessly through life. And they have a sense of where they're going, what their success is going to look like. They seem happy and fulfilled, because they are.

Sounds good, eh? And the best news is, you can be just like them. They aren't achieving this by virtue of some innate talent they were just born with. They're using skills we can all learn. I've watched them, and I know what they do. And if you read this book, you'll know it too. I've spent time analysing what they do differently, and I've identified eight key areas where they're proactively taking control of their lives, removing the obstacles in their way, and creating a clear path towards whatever it is that really matters to them.

Of course some of these Rules are easily understood and much harder to put into practice. I don't claim they're all a piece of cake. In fact, you may already recognise many of them but have struggled to implement them – some of them are common sense, but no less important for that. Where I can, I've tried to suggest ways to incorporate them into everyday life. But in the end I'm just the messenger. I'm passing on what I know works, and it's down to you to make it happen. The next couple of pages also give you some ideas for becoming a fully paid-up Rules Player.

The Rules that follow reveal the secrets to living in a way that puts you in charge of your life, your environment, your destiny. It's your life, and it's time to take control of it so you can focus your effort where it will mean the most and create your own success – whatever that looks like for you. I would say good luck but, if you're following these Rules, luck will be an optional extra.

Richard Templar

How to use the Rules

It can be a bit daunting to read a book with 100 or so Rules for a happier more successful life. I mean, where do you start? You'll probably find you follow a few of them already, but how can you be expected to learn dozens of new Rules all at once and start putting them all into practice? Don't panic, you don't have to. Remember, you don't *have* to do anything – you're doing this because you want to. Let's keep it at a manageable level so you go on wanting to.

You can go about this any way you like, but if you want advice, here's what I recommend. Go through the book and pick out three or four Rules that you feel would make a big difference to you, or that jumped out at you when you first read them, or that seem like a good starting point for you. Write them down here:

Just work on these for a couple of weeks until they've become ingrained and you don't have to try so hard with them. They've become a habit. Great stuff, well done. Now you can repeat the exercise with a few more Rules you'd like to tackle next. Write them here:

Excellent. Now you're really making progress. Keep working through the Rules at your own pace – there's no rush. Before long you'll find you're really getting on top of all the Rules that will help you, and more and more of them are becoming ingrained. And voilà, congratulations – you're a proper Rules Player.

FINANCES

You might define success in terms of how much money you have, in which case making your finances work well for you is essential to your sense of achievement. And even if your own definition of success isn't measured on a financial scale, it's harder to focus your energy where you need to if you're constantly having to watch the pennies.

It's not just the things you can't do and can't have when you don't have the money. It's the constant gnawing in your stomach, the endless worry about paying this bill or that, the sick feeling you wake up with every morning knowing that your outgoings are way too high relative to your income, and you just don't know how to get a handle on it. Oh yes, I've been there.

You don't have to be a millionaire. Dammit, you don't even need savings in the bank some months – you'd settle for just being able to pay the bills, feed the kids, stay afloat. Mind you, as soon as you have money, you increase your commitments – we all do it. You get a more expensive rental flat or a bigger mortgage, you buy a car, you go on holiday, you decide you can afford kids now . . . all of which means that even on a decent salary you can still find yourself stressed about how to cover your costs.

I've written before, in *The Rules of Wealth*, about how to set yourself on track for serious money. Right now though, I'm focused on how to manage your money so you can be successful in the broadest sense. What you really want is for your money to grow and flourish alongside the rest of your life. Much better to take charge of your finances from the start, and stay in control of them. That way you know where you are, you can see where you're going, and you've cleared the headspace to succeed in the rest of your life. That's what the next few Rules are all about.

Work out what money means to you

Most of us want plenty of money, for all sorts of reasons. There will be lists of things you'd love to buy or do if only you had more of it, from holidays and cars and houses down to smaller luxury items. You want to be able to spend more on the kids, or to afford to buy cartons of orange juice for everyday consumption,* or to get a new set of curtains for the living room. Unless you're a nun or a hermit – or a billionaire – you'll have some kind of wish list.

But money is important to most of us on a deeper level. It's not just the individual items, it's what money in its overall sense does for you. What are the abstract things it buys you? For some people, for example, the answer to that is security. Having money in the bank means they don't have to worry. They know they'd cope if the landlord kicked them out or if their child had some rare illness that could only be treated abroad, or they could manage fine for at least a year if they were made redundant. If this is you, the thing you really want to do with any extra money is not spend it. You need savings to feed your need for security.

Most of us would like to be in that position, but some of us have a stronger need for money in other ways. Maybe it buys you freedom – it means you can afford to stop living in your parents' house, or you can stick two fingers up to a job you hate, or work only six months of the year. Yes security is all very nice, but if you're not a natural worrier then freedom might be higher up your priority list.

Or how about feeling successful? Some people subconsciously measure their success in life by how much they earn. This book

---

* That's the thing I remember friends having when I was young, which my mother said we couldn't afford

is all about success and, while you might feel successful if you can live modestly but with enough in the bank that you don't need to worry, equally you might feel you're successful only if you have a well-paid job. Your savings are not so much for a rainy day, as for what they say about you and your career. That could be about your personal feeling of achievement, or maybe it's a status symbol that enables you to feel you belong, or makes your parents happy.

You could be at a stage where you'd love to have kids but don't feel you can afford to without the whole family being really hard up. So being able to find, save, generate extra income means you can have a family. Or maybe you crave a bit of luxury in your life – perhaps you've never had it, or perhaps you've grown accustomed to it – and it's that lifestyle that really matters to you. Luxury might mean holidays in top hotels, or it might mean going round the supermarket without having to think about the cost at the checkout. Only you can answer these questions.

Maybe you want money to spare for a mix of these reasons or for some other reason entirely. Unless you become a multi-millionaire there will always be a wish list. If you know what any extra money is really giving you at heart – security, freedom, status, kids, luxury – it makes it much easier to prioritise that wish list in the way that will bring you the most benefit whenever you do have money to spare.

> # UNLESS YOU'RE A NUN OR A HERMIT – OR A BILLIONAIRE – YOU'LL HAVE SOME KIND OF WISH LIST

Know your money

It simply isn't possible to stay in control of your finances if you don't know them intimately. So if you want to live in a world where there are no nasty surprises money-wise, where you have the money you need each month and aren't left wondering where it all went a fortnight before your next pay cheque comes in, this Rule is the foundation to build everything else on.

Money worries just eat away at you, and make it impossible to focus or feel cheerful about anything else that's important to you. So let's make sure you're never in that position again. Even if you have only enough to get by on for the moment, at least you can make sure that you *do* get by without falling into debt.*

If I were to ask you how much you spend each month on, say, socialising – do you know the answer? You should do. OK, each month isn't exactly the same, but you should know the average and have an awareness of whether this month is looking typical or is up or down on the usual spend. And you should be able to answer this question for everything else that needs money too – food shopping, travel, clothes, kids, hobbies, the garden, the car. You may notice that the thing all those examples have in common is that they're not fixed amounts.

It's not so hard to know what your salary is or what your regular insurance or pension amounts are. Those are the easy bits. But you have to know everything if you're going to keep on top of things. We all know those months when you suddenly realise, way later than you'd have liked, that things are going awry. Well, they don't have to happen. If you can answer all those questions about your usual outgoings, you'll realise much sooner that this is a costly month for travel or regular shopping. And you'll be able to take avoiding action in time to avert a money panic.

---

* By the way, if we're too late and you're already flailing financially, there will be Rules later on that will help

Incidentally, if you're self-employed and your income isn't steady, it's much harder to make sure you stay in the black and are able to relax about money. That makes it all the more essential that you follow this Rule, and at least know everything it's possible to know. That way you'll be able to find savings more easily if your earnings are down this month. After all, how can you know where to economise if you don't know what you're spending?

Be ruthless with yourself. If you allow yourself to guess, coast, estimate, leave it to chance in any area of expenditure, you're not doing this Rule properly. We'll look at how to assemble and use all this information later, but the important lesson here is that you recognise the need to know what you're doing with your money, including some of the things you prefer not to think about: Tobacco? Clothes? Alcohol? Chocolate? Takeaways?

You can't bury your head in the sand about your finances because that is the path to ruin. However scary or embarrassing or complicated, you need this information in black and white.

> # HOW CAN YOU KNOW WHERE TO ECONOMISE IF YOU DON'T KNOW WHAT YOU'RE SPENDING?

Reckon your outgoings

You need to know how much you spend, we've just established that. So now you need to find a way to keep track of it. Yes, it is a bit of a faff. Some people love lists and spreadsheets, but if you're not one of them I'm not going to pretend this won't feel a bit like a chore. But listen, once it's done, it will be pretty simple to keep on top of it. And however much of a sinking feeling you get at the prospect of doing it, isn't it better than the sinking feeling you get when you realise you're going into debt?

Anyway, let's minimise the hassle by picking the best way to keep track of your money before you start (so you don't have to switch systems later). You'll know best what works for you, so long as you think about it first and don't just dive into the first thing that comes to mind. The more comfortable you are with the system you use, the easier it will be.

Here are a few options, but this isn't an exhaustive list so you can look around for others, or dream them up for yourself. You might want to keep your information in longhand or on a computer. You can make a list or a table and put regular monthly expenditure next to each item (food, fuel, travel and so on). Another option is to put it all on a spreadsheet. If you like these, it's an excellent system. Some banking apps will tell you where your money is going and will break it down for you by day, week, month or whatever you want. There's personal finance software or apps for your phone. These are great if you're comfortable with the technology, but good old pen and paper is fine if that's what you feel at home with.

You're going to list everything by category, not individual item of expenditure, but make sure your categories are specific enough to be useful. So 'food shopping' is fine – no need to write down exactly what you spend on cereal, or flour – but it's a good idea to separate out supermarket food shopping from takeaway meals, because that's an area you might want to keep track of individually.

The idea here, obviously, is not to have a pretty list. The idea is to identify where your spending is higher than it needs to be so you can economise if and when you need to. Bear that in mind and it will help you to list things in few enough categories to be manageable, but enough to be as useful as possible. To some extent that's a personal thing – you might want to break down regular shopping into food and alcohol. Or not, if your spending on alcohol to drink at home isn't significant. Similarly you might find yourself splitting out different transport costs, or not.

Some items come up only occasionally, or irregularly, so don't forget to include those. Car and house insurance, for example, if you pay them annually – so you need to be able to see ahead that the month they come up for renewal will be a heavy one for outgoings. Christmas can be expensive, and you need to allow for those irregular things through the year like birthdays or kids' school uniform. Your system needs to show you clearly that there's a spike in purchases ahead of the kids' birthdays or that your energy costs go up in winter.

Once you have this regular system, you can see where your money is going. And that's exactly the information you need if you have to make changes because you aren't covering your bills, or you aren't managing to put aside what you need to. Knowledge is power.

> **KNOWLEDGE IS POWER**

RULE 4

Keep checking

The mistake some people make is to go through this process once, and then put their nice list away, or file the document and never look at it again. You're not going to make that mistake.

Your first draft is going to be wrong. You'll have missed things off or underestimated the costs (maybe even overestimated if you're lucky). Your information so far will appear to tell you that you have a certain amount left to play with at the end of the month (let's be positive). But you'll have forgotten that subscription renewal that only comes up once a year, or you won't have allowed for the fact that once a month you do a bigger weekly shop or whoops, how could you have missed off your trips to the cinema (the popcorn as well as the tickets)?

Also you forgot the possibility that the car would break down and need costly repairs, or your laptop would crash and you'd have to buy a new one, or you'd have to pay the pest control people to come and remove a hornet's nest from your house.* You can't budget for these things individually, but after a while you get a sense of the contingency figure you need in a typical month.

And things change. The rent goes up, insurance goes up, your fuel costs go up because you start driving to your parents twice a week while your dad's ill, the kids start going to swimming lessons, work moves you to a different branch and your commute gets more expensive. If you're really lucky, once in a while one of your costs might even go down.

All these things have to be noted down, and your costs updated accordingly. To begin with you'll be amending your notes so often you wonder what the point of it is. But it will settle down quickly, and you'll get into the habit of thinking 'Ah, if I'm going to subscribe to this I must make a note' or whatever.

---

* Yep, happened to me just this month

Have a set time when you sit down and go through your document, or look at what your app or bank or spreadsheet is telling you. That might be once a week or once a month – depending on how much it varies, and probably how tight your budget is too. Always do it on a Friday afternoon, or a Sunday night, or on the train to work on a Tuesday morning. The time doesn't matter, but the routine does. Otherwise it won't happen. The more your costs fluctuate, the more often you need to do this in order to make sure it's a quick minor adjustment each time – easy to keep on top of – and not a massive chore three or four times a year.

You need to do this because not only will it tell you where you are now, but you can use this information to put yourself in a better place in future. This is the foundation of your financial success – the oracle that tells you where you can economise, because that's the basis of being able to save, and build your financial reserves. There's the money for your better car, your dream holiday, your own house, your early retirement.

> **THIS IS THE FOUNDATION OF YOUR FINANCIAL SUCCESS**

Knowing where you stand is half the battle

If your earnings are comfortable and your outgoings steady, you might feel satisfied with the way your finances are looking right now. Many of us, though, would like the accounts to be looking healthier. Even if you're surviving OK, you'd like more money for one reason or another. And maybe you're barely even surviving – lots of people have been there at least at certain times in their lives. It's a scary feeling, not knowing how long you can go on making ends meet.

The huge temptation is to bury your head in the sand. Of course it is, because if you raise it you might see the bills and costs coming down the road straight at you. Who wants to look at that? How much easier to pretend it isn't there, that it might all be OK, you might win the lottery . . . Incidentally, have you added up what you've spent on lottery tickets over the years, and set it against what you've won? The probability of coming out ahead is statistically negligible. When you buy a lottery ticket you buy hope. That's all. If you recognise that, and can spare the money, then carry on. But from a financial standpoint you have to budget it as a cost, and one you may not be able to afford.

From a psychological perspective, if you're up against it financially, you have to look straight down the barrel of the metaphorical gun. Be brave, grit your teeth, take a big gulp and face up to every last bit of spending, every bill coming up in the next few weeks and months, every last cost. And assume only the income that is guaranteed – don't budget for possible windfalls that may never happen. It's always better once there are no surprises, however bad things look.

So be brutal with yourself about those things we've been discussing, about getting everything down on paper, in a spreadsheet, in your app. And you know what? However scary, there's something quite cathartic about looking the worst in the face. About knowing your enemy. Once you remove the element of surprise, you have the upper hand.

You might need to take urgent action, or get professional help, and facing up to the facts is the first step to doing that. I hope, however, that you reach this point in time to avert disaster and to find ways to reduce your spending, or perhaps increase your income.

If you're in a relationship or living with family, you'll need to make sure that your partner or anyone else who spends the household money is also fully aware of the need to economise. This isn't always easy, but you need to have the conversation. There's no point you saving money just so someone else can spend it on non-essentials. Both of you – or all of you – need to know where you stand.

> ## ONCE YOU REMOVE THE ELEMENT OF SURPRISE, YOU HAVE THE UPPER HAND

Stick to notes

Depending on how young you are, you might remember the old days when almost all transactions took place in cash, with perhaps the occasional cheque (remember them?) for larger sums. The reason electronic payments took over when the technology was developed was because it's much simpler, easier, more efficient and often more secure.

But there is a downside. It's easier to spend money now in every sense. It's not just that the process is simpler, it's also that tapping a bit of plastic on the side of a machine doesn't make the money feel as real as it did when we used to count out notes and coins.

I know plenty of people older than me* who still prefer to stick to the old ways. And interestingly, they are among the most frugal people I know, even though most of them no longer have to be as careful as they did when they had young families, for example. There are several reasons for this obviously, and some are cultural – to do with their upbringing for instance – but one of the reasons is that they deal in cash and they can see what they're spending. So they regularly question whether they really need to buy this or that.

Younger people on a tight budget are starting to see the sense in this. One option when things are tight is to switch to cash only. The benefit of this is entirely psychological – it doesn't change your income – but it can have a significant effect for many people. Once you can see your money, it's harder to spend it.

The idea is that when your weekly or monthly salary is paid, you draw it out of your account in cash. You can divide it up according to your outgoings, setting aside a portion for food shopping, or rent, or bills, or going out, or wherever your money goes. You can see what you have, and once the relevant file or envelope is

---

* Yes, there are still some left

empty, you can't spend any more. This system – obviously you have to stick to it properly – will prevent you from just spending a few quid here or there on things you don't really need. With a debit card, you can do that without really noticing, but if you can see the remaining money in that pile disappearing, it makes you think twice.

I know there are some places now that don't take cash. So you have a section of cash allocated to 'plastic spending' and if you have to buy a coffee on your card, you put the equivalent cash into a pot to go back into your bank account. Equally, some places now work on a cash-only system – to avoid the charges they have to pay on cards – so you could seek these out and spend your cash there.

The great thing with this system is that not only can it help when you're in a tight spot and need to rein in your spending, it's also a great way to save when things aren't quite so tight.

> ## ONCE YOU CAN SEE YOUR MONEY, IT'S HARDER TO SPEND IT

Be honest

For some reason it's always been considered taboo to discuss what you earn with other people. It's a bit daft really, considering you can get a pretty good idea by looking at where and how people live, the car they drive, how they dress, what they do for a living. Nevertheless, it's traditionally not the done thing to talk about it openly, at least not in my part of the world.

However, if your finances are stretched, one of the trickiest problems can be other people's expectations. Friends who – presumably – are better off than you at the moment will suggest evenings out that you can't really afford. Your family will suggest all clubbing together to rent a holiday place for a get-together. Your best mate wants everyone to stump up for a hen night or stag do.

It's easy to feel under pressure to join in, or unable to say that the plans are out of your budget. However, these things can be a big financial drain. Even an evening out that only stretches your budget a little can become unaffordable when you go out with friends every week.

Actually, though, how would you feel if one of your friends or family responded to a suggestion from you by saying, 'I'd love to but unfortunately it's out of my budget at the moment'? Assuming you're a Rules Player, you'd be entirely understanding and sympathetic. And if your friends are half as lovely as you, why wouldn't they respond the same way? My view is that anyone who doesn't react positively doesn't deserve your consideration anyway, but I'd be surprised if you met many of those. Most people have been there at some point, and they'll understand.

You don't have to say you're really strapped at the moment if you don't feel comfortable with that – or if it's not true and you simply prefer to spend your money elsewhere. I have one friend who declines expensive suggestions by saying (truthfully) that they're saving for a deposit on a flat at the moment. There might be a few occasions when your friends or family go ahead without you, as well as times they modify their plans to fit your budget. Don't take it personally – they have as much right to splash out as you do to economise – and think of the money you've saved.

It can help to be creative about ways to socialise on a budget. If you can suggest a less expensive evening out or holiday that's just as much fun for everyone, why wouldn't they agree? A family picnic, or a games evening at someone's flat, or renting an old favourite move and making popcorn, instead of a pricey trip to the cinema.

> MOST PEOPLE HAVE BEEN
> THERE AT SOME POINT, AND
> THEY'LL UNDERSTAND

Take account of your mindset

Rule 6 was about using cash only, because it's harder to spend it without noticing. You need to take your own psychology into account when you want to get to grips with your spending, so that money stops being a negative in your life and – hopefully – starts to become a positive. So anything that slows you down before you spend, makes you stop and think, can only be a good thing.

So here's a suggestion that can work alongside the cash-only strategy, or in place of it for anyone who finds dealing in cash only just too much to cope with (or lives miles from the nearest cash machine). How about opening another bank account, or even two, to help you curb unnecessary spending? I'm not advocating having dozens of bank accounts – I'd stick to single figures – but an extra account or two can be very handy.

Here's an example of why I do it myself. I'm freelance, so I pay my own tax. And here in the UK there's currently quite a lag between earning the money and sending the tax to the Inland Revenue. So I put a percentage of everything I earn, as soon as it comes in, into a separate bank account to cover the amount I'm going to be taxed on it – eventually. That way, when the tax bill comes in, I know I'll have the money to cover it. I don't touch that account for anything else. That takes a huge load off my mind, and I don't have to worry about being unable to meet my tax bill.

I know several people who have a mobile banking account, which they use for everyday spending. They transfer a set amount into it at the start of the month, and that's their everyday spending money. They continue to pay bills and so on from their high street bank account. I would just say that most mobile banks are perfectly able to handle all your banking, so the people who do this are simply tapping into the psychological advantage of being able to separate their money into different pots. You could just as well achieve the same thing by having two different accounts with the same bank – and some people go for this option.

Another variation is to calculate how much all your regular direct debits and standing orders come to, and then create an account to pay them all from. Obviously at the start of each month, or when your pay cheque comes in, you pay the amount you'll need into this account. That means all your regular bills – rent, mortgage, utilities, insurances – are covered so you don't need to worry about them.

You need to think through how your own mind works to decide which (if any) of these strategies will work for you. There are plenty of options, and you may want to use a couple of them. All of them mean you can stop worrying about a chunk of your money because you've ring-fenced it in a really visible way. For lots of us this is much easier than having some nebulous rule that we won't spend more than this or that on certain things. Like cash, it's visible so you know where you are. And crucially, it takes a huge amount of the worry out of your finances and frees you to get on with your life.

> **ANYTHING THAT SLOWS YOU DOWN BEFORE YOU SPEND, MAKES YOU STOP AND THINK, CAN ONLY BE A GOOD THING**

Save where you can

If you're serious about saving money, you can find ways to cut your costs. Then put those savings towards staying afloat or, if you can, build a savings pot towards the things that are really important to you. If you're not quite at that stage yet, at least you can save a fund for contingencies so you aren't left struggling next time there's an unexpected bill.

Listen, there are lots of websites and other advice out there giving advice on ways to save money, and many of them are excellent. The challenge for you is to find the motivation. That might not be difficult if you're seriously in debt. However if you have money, just not as much as you'd like, it can be harder to make it happen. If you take this seriously you could save literally thousands. There's no question it's worth it. You just need to stop thinking about it and get on with it.

So turn it into a kind of game. Make it a project you can get your teeth into. You can very broadly divide up money-saving strategies into two groups. There are the savings that require you to change things pro-actively, and the ones that come from changing your lifestyle and habits.

The first group includes switching energy accounts, bank accounts, insurance, cancelling subscriptions, and so on. So set aside a few hours to go through all your utilities and see if you can't get the same thing cheaper elsewhere. Or even phone up providers and ask if they can offer you a cheaper deal – it always amazes me how much you can save this way. I recently got around £20 a month off a utility bill simply by phoning them. Multiply that over a whole year, and several utilities, and you can see how easy it can be to get into four-figure savings. It might seem like a tedious process, but if you go through everything in one go you'll have it all sorted in a day or so.

Now look at any subscriptions you have. Lots of people these days subscribe to only one TV streaming channel at a time, watch everything they want to and then cancel the subscription and take out a new one with a different channel. I used to buy a daily newspaper and stopped when I realised the only thing I really wanted was the puzzles pages – I could get the news free online – so I subscribed to the puzzles only for the cost of buying about one paper a month. Conversely, if you buy the same magazine every week or month anyway, a subscription would be cheaper than picking it up at the shop. So think about all your subscriptions and question whether there isn't a better way.

Lifestyle changes can be trickier. The whole thing about changing habits is that it feels like an effort until the new habit is ingrained. But that only takes a few weeks, and you can start with the things that feel most achievable, and add other tweaks once you can see the difference. Obviously the big winners here are things like quitting smoking and alcohol, but there's lots of money to be saved by turning off lights, turning the heating down by one degree, walking or cycling instead of driving, using coupons and vouchers, and so on. It all adds up.

Oh, and avoid temptation. Don't shop when you're hungry. In fact, maybe don't shop. Buy groceries online so you can't browse, and don't look at new clothes or books or whatever your weakness is. Block notifications and unsubscribe from mailing lists so online shops and takeaways can't thrust temptation under your nose. Before you know it, your spending will plummet and your savings account will be looking lush.

> SO TURN IT INTO A KIND OF
> GAME. MAKE IT A PROJECT
> YOU CAN GET YOUR TEETH
> INTO

Plan the route

So you've got your finances into the best shape you can, and you know exactly what's what. You're tracking your expenditure, and you know where every penny is going. So what now? You want to be successful financially – whatever you've decided that means to you – and you want to be able to focus on achieving your goals in the rest of your life without having to worry about money.

Now you need to do some hard thinking. Money doesn't just arrive in our laps without effort, so you need to be precise and targeted about what money you're going to need and how you'll get it. Let's assume, for the sake of argument, that you're not going to win the lottery. Nor is any distant relative going to die and leave you everything. No, if you're going to have more money in ten years' time than you have now, you're going to have to make it happen yourself. Far too many people go through life without ever quite getting to where they want to be, because they rely on hope rather than concrete plans. Don't be one of them.

So make yourself a wish list of what you want the money for. Not a pie-in-the-sky list of super yachts and villas in the south of France. Maybe one day – if you do win the lottery – but let's not run before we can walk. What are the things you can't afford now that might be attainable, and that you really want in the future? For example, do you want eventually to buy your own home? Are you hoping to start a family if you can afford it? Maybe you have an all-consuming hobby and would love to work only three or four days a week. These are reasonable aspirations for most of us, and achievable if we really want to put in the effort.

Suppose you could save £20 every week. That's around £1k per year. What could you do with that in five years' time? And what if you could save £50 a week? Or more? It's surprising how fast money can build up if you give it a chance. Yes, you'll have to give something up – but you're giving it up in order to live somewhere better, or to have kids, or to fund something that will make a big difference to your life in the long term. Now you know exactly where you are financially, you can start to look at where you can make savings. How are you going to fund your wish list? That question should be much easier to answer now.

Once you do the sums, you might reckon it will take you 50 years to find a deposit for a house. Ah, but that's on your current income and expenditure. What if your income goes up? Once you can see all the figures, and you know you'll need more money, you can start planning how to acquire it. No, no, not the lottery. But you could change jobs, retrain for a better-paid job, take on extra work, set up an online shop, do car boot sales, work more hours. I'm not saying you have to do any of these things – it depends how much money you want, and how much you want it. But these are all options, and the joy of having all your finances visible in front of you is that you can plan, talk with your partner or family and create a route map that will take you from where you are now, to where you want to be.

With a clear plan, and figures that you know work, it becomes much easier to focus your spending where it's needed, and easier to say 'no thanks' to anything that will divert you from your dreams.

> ## MONEY DOESN'T JUST ARRIVE IN OUR LAPS WITHOUT EFFORT

RULE 11

Don't chase your own tail

When I was in my late 20s I owned my own house, had three children and a decent job. Money was tight but we got by. By the time I was in my late 30s I had been promoted and my pay had gone up significantly. I owned a bigger house, still had three children, and money was tight but we got by. Then my marriage broke up, the recession hit, my mortgage was worth more than the house and I lost everything.*

In hindsight, although I was unlucky with the timing of the breakup and the recession, a lot of the problem was that every time my income went up, I raised my outgoings – because I could, I suppose. Every raise meant a bigger house, a better car, a more expensive holiday. I didn't think about it at the time. It was just what you did if you could afford it.

Well, it's certainly one option. And if what you really want is a bigger house or more holidays, that's fine. It's your money and you can do what you like with it, and those are valid ways to spend it. However, while your assets might increase this way (barring recession), your disposable income doesn't. You still don't have any more money left at the end of the week to pay the bills or go out on a Friday night.

Go back to what money means to you. What do you really want from it? Security, better holidays, freedom, a more expensive lifestyle, status? You might decide that putting your money into a bigger house will give you what you want. But don't do it blindly like I did. Think about whether you'd prefer to keep your outgoings as they are and save the money – for something special, for the kids, for your retirement, for a sense of security.

---

* Except the three kids of course, who to be fair were worth more than all the rest

These should be conscious decisions. Are you happy on this treadmill? Of course, financially speaking, there's a world of difference between putting your money into an asset that should increase in value – like a house – and spending it on something you won't get back, such as a holiday. Neither is right or wrong, better or worse, smarter or dumber. But they should be deliberate choices.

If you decide to keep your costs as they are when your income goes up, of course you have choices about what to do with the extra money. Save it, spend it on something specific, use it to relax about your everyday spending. It's a great position to be in, so think it through carefully and put that money where it's going to make you feel really good about your life.

> ## ARE YOU HAPPY ON THIS TREADMILL?

RULE 12

Make your money grow

If you really want to feel successful financially, or just want to stop worrying about money so you can enjoy life properly, you want your money to increase while you're not even looking. There are lots of ways to do this, and I'm not going to give you individual advice here. However there are some principles it's wise to follow.

Any money you have built up, and which you don't need to spend again in a hurry, will work harder for you if you put it somewhere other than your high street bank. Bank savings accounts are great for money you'll need to spend again soon, or a bit of an emergency buffer. However you'll always do better in the longer term investing it elsewhere.

Unless you absolutely know what you're doing, find an expert you can trust to manage your money for you. Pick a reputable independent financial advisor, who is accredited by the right regulatory bodies, and pay them. Anyone else is dodgy and too good to be true. Have a clear conversation with them about what you want from your money and what level of risk you are (or aren't) comfortable with. If you opt for relatively low risk, which makes sense for a lot of us, don't complain when they haven't doubled your money in a year – be realistic about what you're trying to achieve. If you opt for high risk, don't complain when you lose a big chunk of your wealth. That's how it goes.

Of course, you could put your money into fixed assets instead. Anything that will go up in value pretty reliably: art, wine, property, that sort of thing. I don't include the house you're living in as you can't sell it without becoming homeless, although you could size up now with a plan to downsize later. Most of these kinds of investments can go down in value in the short term, so they're best used for money you're confident you won't need to get at for a few years. I've known people make huge gains by investing in wine, although you do need to know your wine or your art to invest in them confidently.

If you're someone who worries about the future, a private pension is a great way to feel secure about what happens when you stop work. Potentially it might even be your ticket to early retirement. Remember that once you put money into a pension fund you can't get it back until it matures. On the other hand, when you eventually reach pension age, boy will you be glad you did it. You'll need to weigh this up not only in terms of why and when you most want to get at your money, but also what other pension provision you do or don't have through your work.

Most of us, if we're lucky enough to reach this point, opt for some kind of combination of the above. We don't necessarily do all these things, but we use more than one way to increase our money, and we each have our own balance of what we want to put where. The real Rule is to think hard about what you want from your money, and when you want it, before you decide how to make it work harder.

> **THINK HARD ABOUT WHAT YOU WANT FROM YOUR MONEY, AND WHEN YOU WANT IT**

RELATIONSHIPS

For many of us, other people are what make life worth living. Our families, close friends, social occasions, other people's warmth and approval, those are the things that matter to us. Don't just take my word for it – there's plenty of scientific research to back this up. Some of us much prefer work that gives us plenty of opportunity for inter-action, or choose to spend our free time joining teams or clubs or otherwise hanging out with other people. Even for those of us who enjoy space and privacy, and maybe find socialising can sometimes be challenging, the right relationships are nevertheless vital.

When things are going well, these relationships are a huge positive contribution to our lives. So we want to keep them that way and not let them get in the way, or add to any feelings of stress, overload or unhappiness that make it harder for us to focus on the things that enrich our lives.

You want your romantic partner to be a positive force in your life, but there are times when the relationship can sap your energy. The same goes for your kids, much as you love them. Friends and work colleagues can either energise or drain you, and too many social commitments may leave you struggling to cope. Of course other people will always take up your time, and that's what a big chunk of your time is for. But when they take up more time than you have, or take it up in ways that leave you exhausted and stressed, it's hard to feel in control of your life, and to maintain a healthy balance. When the quantity, or the quality, of the relationships you're juggling start to take over your life, you need to get back in charge.

The following Rules are about how to adjust the relationships you want to keep so that they work for you and not against you, and how to prune those that just aren't worth it.

RULE 13

Recognise social overload

Scientists don't entirely agree about the number of friendships one person can maintain. You might have heard of Dunbar's number, which puts it at 150, but other anthropologists have argued figures closer to 300. I'd have thought it was obvious that we're all different, and indeed that our capacity to maintain friendships varies according to circumstance. However, what is certain is that it's impossible to stay in touch with everyone you've ever wanted to. We all have a personal limit.

It's not difficult to keep in touch with loads of people via Christmas cards or on a social media platform where you don't have to communicate directly for decades yet still have a sense of what each other is up to. That's all fine, but what about the friends you actually see regularly? That might be mates you go out for an evening with, fellow members of a club or group that you belong to, people you take on some kind of caring role for, colleagues you routinely stop for a natter with. Some people might feel they don't get enough human contact, but others can start to feel it becomes quite demanding and hard to fit in around work, family or other commitments.

Too many friends is a thing. It really is. It's not personal – it's just that if you add new friends faster than you drift apart from others, the numbers will grow. And in a busy life, that can start to get in the way. You want to be able to focus on your work, your kids, your passions, and lovely as all these people are, the sheer numbers are making that difficult. How can you nurture the really important relationships in your life if you're being pulled in so many directions?

Look, this happens to most of us, at least at certain times in our lives. The important thing is to understand that it's normal, it's not your fault, and you need to do something about it. If you don't, your social life will take over to the detriment of the rest of your life. If you put off dealing with it, or hope that if you ignore the problem it will go away, what will actually happen is that it will get worse. And worse.

There are plenty of Rules later in this section that will help you to reduce your social interactions. Just to the point where they don't interfere with your other priorities, of course – there's no need to jettison all your friends. As far as this Rule is concerned though, the key is to be clear in your own head that you have a social limit and to recognise when you've reached it.

Stop fighting it. Stop feeling guilty about all the things you imagine you 'should' be doing but can't. Those might be social things you can't squeeze into your diary, or it might be all the other things your social calendar has squeezed out. There are only 24 hours in your day, same as for all of us, and it can be a huge relief when you give yourself permission to reduce the socialising down to a point where you can enjoy everything else too.

> # BE CLEAR IN YOUR OWN HEAD THAT YOU HAVE A SOCIAL LIMIT, AND RECOGNISE WHEN YOU'VE REACHED IT

Be honest about what works

So you've accepted that your social life needs a bit of trimming, in order to give everything else a bit of air to breathe. Well done – that's the first hurdle cleared. Right, now you have to think about which bits to trim.

The key to making this work is to be honest with yourself. This isn't – at this stage – about what you think you *ought* to trim (or keep). It's about being totally clear about which bits of your social life, and which relationships, are actually benefiting you. And which aren't. Time enough later to consider whether something should stay even if you don't enjoy it, or go even if you do. Just now, you need a clear head about this process and the first step to that is understanding what actually fits well into your life without leaving you feeling squeezed.

This will be different for everyone, and indeed it may be different for you now from what it was a year ago, or will be next year. So I can't give you a list – you have to do that bit for yourself.

OK, so think about each of your friendships, relationships and social activities. You can sit down and work it through in your head, or consider each one as you're next on your way to it, or heading home afterwards. What are we trying to do again? That's right, we want your personal and social life to excite and energise you, not to overwhelm you to the point it interferes with your feelings of happiness, success and achievement in other areas.

There's more than one way for these relationships to get in the way. It may be that they collectively take up too much time so you're always exhausted, or you can't fit in other things that matter to you. Or perhaps the time isn't such an issue, but certain relationships are bringing you down, affecting your mood, sapping your energy. Or maybe your friends, much as you enjoy their company, always want to socialise in ways that cost more money than you can spare, so it leaves you worried about finances.

We're still at the thinking stage here, so just work through in your mind which of your relationships gives you a sinking feeling, for any of these reasons – or any other reason. You can't start to streamline your social life so that it feeds you rather than drains you, until you've identified where the problem areas are that you need to address.

Of course this isn't usually a major audit of your relationships. Once you're in the habit of thinking this way, you'll be able to identify the relationships that aren't working before they become routine and head any problems off at the pass. You'll learn to raise the question of your budget with your friends *before* everyone gets in the habit of a meal out every week, or to tell your neighbourhood watch from the off that you're happy to help but you won't have time to sit on the committee.

Once you've got a sense of where the difficult areas are, which are the triggers that are bringing you down, you're in the right place to do something about it. You should be starting to feel a bit lighter.

> # YOU'LL BE ABLE TO IDENTIFY THE RELATIONSHIPS THAT AREN'T WORKING BEFORE THEY BECOME ROUTINE

Know what you want in your life

I hope by now you have a sense of which activities and relationships are enhancing your life, and which aren't. Perhaps you've realised that a lot of your work stress is down to everyone in the office chatting to the point you struggle to get through the day's tasks before 5 o'clock. Or conversely that going for an after-work drink once a week with colleagues doesn't take too much time, and really helps to ease any pressures and let off a bit of steam.

So you can start to assemble a mental wish-list (or you can write it down if you like) of the things you'd like to keep in your life and the things you'd like to prune – we'll look at how you can do that in a moment. For now, you're establishing what you *want* to stop or reduce. Don't jump ahead and start fretting about how to do it.

But here's a tricky one . . . Maybe calling round to your elderly neighbour's every day to help her with everyday tasks is really getting you down. You don't have the time for it, and it's putting you under a lot of pressure. But she's got nobody else, and you feel you have to do it. There might be a few relationships like this on your list. You don't want to give them up – you'd feel worried or guilty or unkind if you did – but they're adding to the strain and putting the rest of your life under pressure.

Look, it's up to you. I'm not telling you to abandon your neighbour. Or to keep calling round. You need to decide whether having your neighbour in your life, at that level, is something you want. Maybe it saps you but you feel it's worth it. Rule 14 was about what works, and this Rule is about what you actually want. They're not the same thing, which is why you need to think through both questions. Maybe your neighbour commitment isn't really helping your life, but it makes you feel good and you want to carry on.

If you wanted to put this down on paper* you could draw a matrix – a 2 × 2 square like this:

	ENJOY	DON'T ENJOY
SHOULD DO		
DON'T HAVE TO DO		

Whether you do this on paper or in your head, you can place all your relationships and activities in one of these four boxes. If you enjoy it and want to do it, it goes in the top left. If you don't enjoy it but want to carry on anyway – because you feel you should for some reason – it goes in the top right, and so on.

At the end of this process, you'll have a top left (mental) box of things that will stay, and a bottom right box of things you can stop doing. Unless the top left box is still so huge it's getting in the way of the rest of your life, the only things you need to think about are the things you enjoy but could easily give up and the ones you don't enjoy but feel you ought to do.

> # RULE 14 WAS ABOUT WHAT WORKS, AND THIS RULE IS ABOUT WHAT YOU ACTUALLY WANT

---

* It's your call – I'm a writer and I wouldn't bother putting it down on paper. It wouldn't help me. But if that's how your brain works, then do it. My wife would. She puts everything down on paper.

Decide what goes

You're making real progress here. You've analysed where your social time is going and which of those activities or people enhance your life. You've also worked out which relationships you really want to keep and which can definitely go. If you've decided to wind down enough of these, you may feel your diary is already giving you back the slack you need. If not, you'll need to work through your last two categories in order to clear a bit more space in your week to focus on your priorities.

Those last two groups of people or activities are the ones you enjoy but could easily say no to and the ones you'd gladly drop but feel you ought to keep up. Let's start with that second group – things you feel you ought to do. That might include, for example, your elderly neighbour who you drop in on every day. Or perhaps you help out at a local charity, or mind your friend's kids after school, or sit on a local committee.

Bear in mind that all of these are things you once didn't do. Maybe you're wishing you hadn't started (and there's a lesson there for avoiding this situation in the future). But evidently you're a good person, and they were manageable when you first took them on, so here we are. The thing is, it's easy to overestimate how necessary it is to continue with this kind of commitment. If you weren't there – or hadn't said yes – these things would have been resolved some other way. What way would that have been?

Look, you're struggling to cope, so it makes no sense for you to be the one to help with other people's struggles. If you step back, most of these things will just resolve themselves. What would happen if you moved out of the area, or spent a fortnight in hospital? In many cases, the solution is just to give plenty of warning. Tell the committee or local charity that work or family commitments mean you have to step back, and give them a couple of months' notice – or whatever seems fair on them, but free up your diary in a timeframe you can handle.

That will work for your childminding duties too, with enough warning. And what about your neighbour? Maybe you can find another volunteer to split the duties with or call in every other day. You'll be no use to her if you end up miserable and burnt out, so be fair to both of you, not just her. She might turn out to be fine about it.

I have a friend who had an old pony no one rode any more. It shared a field with another friend's pony, and they helped each other out caring for them. My friend was desperate to rehome her pony, who took an hour or so of her time every day, but felt she'd be letting her friend down. Finally, after several years, she broached the subject – only to discover her friend had been feeling exactly the same way. See? You might be worrying about nothing.

Our last category of relationships is those you enjoy but could stop. And the solution here is pretty simple. If you cut things out of your life that you don't enjoy, the reward is that you've freed up enough time to carry on with the things you love without becoming overloaded. You can always cut things down a bit too – for example see your friend every other week, but maybe with a phone catch-up* the weeks in between. It's about whatever makes you feel better able to manage your life, so it's really your call what arrangement works.

> # IF YOU STEP BACK, MOST OF THESE THINGS WILL JUST RESOLVE THEMSELVES

---

* I appreciate that if you're under 30 you won't know what this is

Prune respectfully

Let me guess. You've decided what needs to be pruned but you can't work out how to do it? If you found it easy to say no, I doubt you'd be in this position to begin with. So let's suppose you really want to give up or cut down on certain friends or commitments, but you don't feel assertive enough to do it. Let's look at a few options.

The simplest thing is to do nothing. Sometimes simply by not putting your hand up, you can remove the problem. That committee where no one else ever seems to step forward? Just do the same as the rest of them, and don't step forward. A lot of friends can be pruned by just leaving the ball in their court. I don't mean ghosting them (obviously – you're a Rules Player), I just mean leave *them* to suggest the next lunch date or evening out each time. Doesn't work for everyone, but for some it's a great way to move them from a regular catch-up to an occasional one.

In other cases, you need to have a friendly but firm conversation. Just be honest. Let them know you're fairly overloaded at the moment, and you need to meet up a bit less often, or step down from the organising committee, or pop round every *other* day, or be strict about not allowing yourself to chat during work time (save it for lunch or after work). Tell your friends that your budget is a bit tight and you'd love to see them every week but for now the activity needs to be affordable. You'd be surprised how understanding most people are – and some may even be grateful if they're in the same boat.

Oh, and stop saying yes to things. I know it can feel really uncomfortable saying no, but if you don't learn how to, you'll be right back here in another few months. You're perfectly entitled to say a polite no, without explanation, and leave it at that. But if you find that difficult, just come up with a way to soften it: 'Oh, I'd have loved to, but I really don't have time', or 'I'm sorry I can't, but have you tried asking Ali?' (Don't just dump Ali in it here, but maybe they will be able to help, or they're just better at saying no.)

Always keep in mind why you're doing this. It's because you want to spend more time with your partner or kids, or you need to give your elderly parents more support, or your career is flagging because you can't focus on it, or you feel exhausted and stressed too much of the time. Tell yourself this before you say no, and you may find it a little easier.

You want to be a success, someone who achieves the targets they set themselves, a person who knows how to focus on the things that matter in life. Remember that, before you have a conversation you think may be tricky, and steel yourself. And you know what? Most of the time the conversation will go absolutely fine, and you'll wonder what you were worried about.

> # IT CAN FEEL REALLY UNCOMFORTABLE SAYING NO, BUT IF YOU DON'T LEARN HOW TO, YOU'LL BE RIGHT BACK HERE IN ANOTHER FEW MONTHS

You don't have to socialise

It's easy to fall into the trap of thinking that you have to put time into socialising just because other people are doing it. Maybe your team likes to go for a drink after work, or your family meets up every Sunday, or the school parents always go for coffee after drop-off. Going along with these arrangements is the easy thing to do, but it's not the only option.

When you start to feel the pressure elsewhere in your life, and need to free up some breathing space, it's OK to excuse yourself from these meet-ups. You won't be the first person ever to skip one. Of course if you enjoy it you won't want to skip too many, but you have to weigh up the effect it's having on the rest of your life. There's no need to go cold turkey and never attend these social events ever again. Just miss the odd one here or there – apart from anything else, it gets people used to you not attending. So then you can cut down further without drawing attention to it. Of course when you have the time and headspace you can go back to it more regularly.

I know people who hate parties. Some of them just never go and, you know what? No one minds. Unless it's maybe your best friend, or your sister, there'll be several people who can't make it. You might imagine that everyone will notice your absence but, actually, very few people will (unless it's your best friend's party, or your sister's). Their focus will be on the people who *are* there, not the ones who aren't.

I'll grant you it can be a bit trickier with family arrangements for some of us. On the other hand, if you're lucky, it might be easier to be assertive with your family. The real trick (no use now, but in future) is not to get caught in the first place. Don't allow anything to become a regular, frequent commitment unless you're very sure you're happy to keep it going. It's easier to see your in-laws once a week at a random time than to see them every Tuesday. That way, you can let it slip a little bit from time to time when you're busy.

Equally, you want to train your family not to expect you to turn up every time they get together for Sunday lunch. Let them know you'd love to be there when you can, but it won't be every time. And Christmas . . . that all too frequently turns into a commitment you can only get out of by dying. The trouble with all these things is that while they might be really enjoyable (or not?), it's the feeling that you *have* to do it that can really put you under pressure when life is very full on. You want to set up scenarios where you turn up to these things when you can, without setting the kind of precedent that makes it impossible ever to say no again.

Incidentally, you can also help by not imposing this kind of pressure on your own family. Let them know it's OK to say no if they're busy, and tell your grown-up kids that they can spend Christmas wherever they like (that way it feels even better when they choose to spend it with you). All this will help to create the kind of family relationships where everyone is free to say no to things without causing an atmosphere – and that benefits you and everyone else.

> **GOING ALONG WITH THESE ARRANGEMENTS IS THE EASY THING TO DO, BUT IT'S NOT THE ONLY OPTION**

Finesse your family

Family are with you for a lifetime and, in most families, you want to be there for each other's ups and downs. But what if someone else's downs coincide with yours? Just when you're feeling stressed or overloaded or under pressure, when your kids are being demanding or your career is stalling, or your health is suffering . . . suppose that's when your daughter's relationship falls apart, or your mum breaks her shoulder and needs help looking after herself, or your brother gets made redundant.

Look, I can't make all these things go away. To some extent a close family will always create demands that you want to be there to help with. That's what family is about when it works. But it doesn't change the fact that it doesn't always come at the best time for you. So how can you mitigate the stress and the detrimental impact on the rest of your life?

The first thing is to think about your priorities. I say this because sometimes, if you think about it, you'll come to the conclusion that this particular family crisis is your priority, and that other things will need to give so you can focus on this (the section on Time, Rules 23–36, will help with this). You might think, 'Aaargh! I don't have time to deal with my daughter/brother/mum's problems' while I'm so busy with this or that. However, seeing this as 'I don't have time to deal with this or that while my daughter/ brother/mum needs me' can really help make room for the things that matter.

I realise you may not always be able to create time and space for family, so here are some other angles to look at. First of all, when time is precious, commit to the least time you can, simply because you can always give more if you feel you need to. If you overcommit, it's much harder to cut down.

Depending on the scenario, it can actually be less work to have an ill member of the family – or a heartbroken one – in your house than to have to make time for them elsewhere. There's no extra catering, and you can check in with them for 30 seconds several times a day, rather than have to take a chunk out of your day to phone or visit. If you have other family in the household, they can help. Even young kids can keep grandma or grandad busy while you get on with other things.

If your adult child, or your brother, keep phoning for moral support or a shoulder to cry on, just turn your phone off occasionally. It will give you much more of a break if you know they can't get hold of you, even if it's just for half an hour's peace while you walk the dog or have a nap. You want to be there for them, yes, but it doesn't have to be 24/7. You can always say 'If I'm busy and my phone is switched off, message me and I'll call when I pick it up'. It can be hard to ignore a message you can see, but with the phone off it's much easier to think about something else.

You have to keep yourself sane and functioning, or you're no use to anyone. So it's not selfish to give yourself these little breaks, it's necessary for everyone. It keeps you fresh so you can focus better on supporting your family's troubles. Maybe the next crisis won't come at such a bad time for you but, for now, the important thing is to find those little strategies that enable you to fit your family's demands alongside everything else.

> **YOU HAVE TO KEEP YOURSELF SANE AND FUNCTIONING, OR YOU'RE NO USE TO ANYONE**

Make proper time for your partner

When you're under pressure, it's often your relationship with your partner that suffers. You niggle at each other, you snap, you get irritated when they end up on your list of people who seem to want time and effort from you. They want you to do school pick-up today, or collect their dry cleaning, or remind them where they left their keys. That irritation is all very natural, and we all do it. It doesn't have to mean your relationship is in trouble, it's just that you (maybe both of you) have too much on your plate to cope with nurturing a relationship at the same time.

Hang on though. If you're lucky enough to be in a broadly good relationship, shouldn't that be your greatest support when you're feeling a bit overwhelmed, and out of control? Isn't your partner the person who can do the most to ease the pressure on you? So how can you turn this around so your relationship is helping rather than hindering you?

The answer is to put more time into it. '*Time*?' I hear you say, 'That's EXACTLY what I don't have right now – have you been listening *at all*?' Yes, I have, and please don't shout at me. Listen, if your relationship is going well, the benefits far outweigh the challenge of finding time for it. Your partner can help you on so many practical and emotional levels that any investment in the relationship will be more than repaid.

So make sure you have uninterrupted time together which you set aside to talk about whatever you need to. All those five minutes while you're doing a million other things don't count – this needs to be time when you're free to look each other in the eye. That might be an evening out once a week – or an evening in if you can prevent interruptions. It might be half an hour each night in bed before sleep. If you can find the energy for sex, that connection will really help too. All this will give you time to offload, reflect, ask advice, ask for help, have a cry, have a laugh, think out loud – whatever will help you feel more in control of your life. How can that not be worth finding time for?

You can talk about the snappiness and irritation that comes from feeling under pressure generally and, between you, you can find ways to circumvent it. Well, most of it. And when it does happen, the fact you've talked about it should help you to find the humour in it, to be more tolerant, to understand where it comes from, not to make it seem personal.

Honestly, if you're in a good relationship, you won't find anywhere better to put your time. Not only because it will help you through and put you back in control of your life, but also because it will strengthen the relationship too. For both of you. Because I hope it's obvious that this goes both ways – sometimes both at the same time. You can both support each other, whoever most needs it at the moment. A strong relationship is a big part of what makes your life successful, and that's true in bad times and good.

> **A STRONG RELATIONSHIP IS A BIG PART OF WHAT MAKES YOUR LIFE SUCCESSFUL**

Focus on quality

When time and energy are at a premium, you need to invest what you have in the right places. Suppose your parents are elderly and need support, but meantime you're overrun at work, the kids are demanding and the dog needs exercising, I've just told you to find more time for your relationship . . . and there still seem to be only 24 hours in a day.

So think hard about what input actually needs to come from you, when your family or close friends want help. Let's take the example of your parents – lots of us reach a point when our parents can't really cope without us, and it often coincides with the demands of kids still at home, and a career that we can't ignore. You might feel you should call in on your parents daily if they're local, or take a whole day out to visit every week or two if they're further afield. But that's a huge chunk of your time.

However, a lot of your parents' needs will be purely practical. Someone needs to do their shopping, or remind them to take their medication, or help with admin, or clean or cook or wash for them. Anyone can do these things – it doesn't have to be you. What they need from you is a good relationship, lots of love and to feel they matter. Those things can't be ticked off a list with one visit a year, but neither do they need several hours a day.

So try to offload as many practical jobs as you can. Are there neighbours who can help? Social services? Other family? Can you do their shopping online for them rather than in person? Of course all these things take time to organise, but once they're in place they could save you hours every week. That will make it easier to phone every day or two, and call in for a decent visit every few days – where you can sit and talk instead of rushing round cleaning or unpacking shopping.

If you find ending a phone call difficult – if your parents are less busy than you they may want to natter for longer than you can spare – call a bit before you have another commitment so you *have* to say 'Got to go, I'm off to pick the kids up from school/I'm going into a meeting/the potatoes are boiling over'.

If you have siblings (in the example of your parents) there may also be tricky conversations about who puts in the time to help. You might think – and you might be right – that your brother or sister isn't pulling their weight. However, they may see things differently. You're in different situations in terms of proximity to your parents, work demands, kids and all the rest. It's human nature to see your own pressures in sharper relief than other people's. So approach other family members with understanding and sympathy. They deserve it, and they're much more likely to co-operate. And you both need to recognise that things change over time, and you may need to rejig in future. If your brother or sister won't put in the time – maybe they live much further away – would they consider a financial contribution instead so you can pay someone to clean or buy in some ready-made meals?

The key to staying on top of these situations is to make sure you're focusing what time you have where it will be most appreciated, and not spending it on things other people could do just as well.

> # WHAT THEY NEED FROM YOU IS A GOOD RELATIONSHIP, LOTS OF LOVE AND TO FEEL THEY MATTER

It's OK to have a break from the kids

My goodness kids can be exhausting. Yes they're adorable, yes they're fascinating, yes you love them but – come on – there are few things more emotionally and mentally draining than spending all day with them. Just because you signed up for it in principle, you can still go through days or even phases where it all feels like too much.

You know those superwomen who seem to have it all – high-flying careers, stunning (and spotless) homes, oodles of clean and charming kids? Pretty much all of them are only achieving it because they have help. Ditto all the similarly successful fathers, although what some of them have is capable partners. It simply isn't possible to find time for a successful career without it, never mind stay sane. While the kids are small enough to need supervising, it's not just helpful to have backup, it's essential.

Of course, that support can take plenty of forms. You don't have to employ a nanny or send your five-year-old to boarding school. If success for you doesn't involve a career, you might manage on your own most of the time. Or you and your partner might share the childcare so you both have some clear space for work. Maybe you earn enough for a bit of childcare, or perhaps you have family nearby who are happy to help.

Even in the best-run system though, there can be times when a crisis of some kind comes along and you find that looking after the kids is just more than you can do and still stay sane. And raising kids is unremitting. When things aren't going well, it can drag you down and take over the rest of your life too. The thing is, the kids are always the top priority. Not necessarily attending to their every whim (and some of them have a lot of whims), but making sure they're safe and their basic needs are catered for overrides everything.

So this Rule is here to remind you that it doesn't always have to be you who does it. You can delegate. Many parents feel guilty about leaving their children in someone else's care, they feel it's their 'job' to look after them personally. But it really isn't. You need to stay sane and have enough headspace to enable the rest of your life to run smoothly too – caring for other relatives, looking after your career, getting the bills paid, running the household. If a regular half day or day a week away from the kids helps, or a few ad hoc days when other things are getting on top of you, that's OK. In fact it's better than OK, because the rest of the time your children will see a happier, more effective you.

What's more, it's really good for them. Whether it's family or a friend or paid childcare, it gives the kids a chance to interact with a different adult. They'll learn loads, they'll be less clingy, it will build their confidence, and if ever you're unavoidably away – a couple of days in hospital, or a major work emergency – they're much better placed to cope without you. So never feel bad about taking the breaks you need to keep you on top of your game. It's good for you, and good for the kids too.

> # WHETHER IT'S FAMILY OR A FRIEND OR PAID CHILDCARE, IT GIVES THE KIDS A CHANCE TO INTERACT WITH A DIFFERENT ADULT

TIME

Successful people know how to make the most of their time. Modern life gives us much more free time than ever before, and more opportunities to enjoy it. On the flip side, this can sometimes make you feel there's just too much to do and not enough hours in the day. It can be overwhelming, can't it? It's not that you necessarily don't enjoy any of the things on your to-do list – there are simply too many of them.

Whether it's work, kids, socialising, finding time to spend with your partner, looking after your parents, walking the dog, helping out at the local club/school/neighbourhood watch, going to the gym, finishing that book you started weeks ago . . . they're all things you wanted to do. But how on earth are you going to find time for them all?

If you're struggling to get everything done without letting anyone down, you'll stop enjoying it. Things that should be fun become a chore. People who take up your time become an irritation. The thought of how you'll fit it all in with only 24 hours in a day becomes depressing and can even make you feel quite panicky.

Well don't panic, because the next few Rules are all about how to get back in control of your diary and your to-do list, and give yourself room to enjoy the things you choose to do with your time. Whether you're already thoroughly overwhelmed, or simply feeling life would go more smoothly if you were less busy, this section is for you.

Know your driver

So why do you take on too much? You might think it's just life, and there's nothing you can do about it. But there are very few people for whom that's actually true. Most of us do it for a reason, even if we don't recognise the reason. And the lucky people who keep busy but don't take on too much are generally the ones who aren't driven by some unconscious need to be busy. It's far easier for them to say no to things, or not volunteer in the first place. So if we can understand our own need to be busy, it will give us a self-awareness that can only help us to change the way we operate.

It would be impossible to give you an exhaustive list of reasons for keeping (too) busy, but I'll give you a few common examples. You may recognise yourself here and, if not, it should help you do a bit of soul-searching to understand what drives your psychological need to overload yourself.

I have a friend who has such a need to be busy that he can't do nothing for even a few minutes. In fact, he struggles to do only one thing at a time. If he's talking to you he'll be doing a sudoku on his phone at the same time, if he invites you for a meal he'll be working while he cooks while he socialises. Not surprisingly, his life is overstuffed with activity and he gets very stressed trying to keep on top of it all. From the outside, it makes no sense – why not do less if he's struggling with the pressure? The answer to that is, for whatever reason, that he can't face being alone inside his head. Instead of addressing (or even recognising) this genuine problem, he compounds it with the pressure of becoming over-loaded and never having enough time.

I had a relative when I was younger who was under-assertive and incapable of saying no to anyone. She took on any task she was asked to, even when it meant staying up all hours to keep on top of things, rather than say 'I'm sorry, I just don't have the time'. Why couldn't she say no? Only she could have answered that question – perhaps she had been raised always to be helpful, or maybe she had a drive to feel needed.

I've encountered many people throughout my life who clearly equate being busy with feeling important. They make a point of letting you know how busy they are because, well, if they're that much in demand they must be important, mustn't they? Personally I've never correlated importance with business, but these people have a need to feel special, in demand, valuable, and want you to see it too. There will be a reason they have this need, and often one that warrants some sympathy, not least because it compels them to live in a state of constant overload.

So think about whether you're unconsciously inviting this state of perpetual overload. Why are you doing it? If you can get to the bottom of it, you can start to address it. It might be a simple lightbulb moment, or you might need help (professional or otherwise) to deal with it, to learn to say no, to recognise you have value without needing other people to see you a certain way, or to be at peace in your own company.

UNDERSTAND WHAT DRIVES YOUR PSYCHOLOGICAL NEED TO OVERLOAD YOURSELF

Itemise your time

I have a weird thing that I think isn't just me. Suppose I have to be somewhere half an hour away at 6 pm. So at 5.30 I head for the front door. And then I don't really know what happens, I enter some kind of parallel universe, and before I know it I haven't actually left the house until 5.40 and I'm going to be ten minutes late. I know it's not just me because I have at least one friend this also happens to (which is quite handy as we're both always ten minutes late).

Obviously, even if I can't explain where those ten minutes go, I still need to factor them in. The thing is, lots of activities take longer than we think. For example, walking the dog for an hour takes more than an hour. Cooking something that takes 30 minutes in the oven takes more than 30 minutes. God knows a 45-minute work meeting can take more than 45 minutes. In some cases the extra time is negligible, but even five or ten minutes – every time – will add up.

If there aren't enough hours in your day, you really can't address the problem until you know where your time is actually going. Not just where you think it's going. So spend a few days tracking what you do and how long it really takes. You can jot it down, keep a spreadsheet, or just note it mentally – whatever works for you. What matters is that you understand where you spend your time, in order to be able to see where you can save it for things you care about more.

You want to be aware where the big items are – commuting, housework, cooking, shopping, work. If the overload is at work, you'll need to break that down into meetings, dealing with emails, breaks, and so on. However, track the smaller items too, and you may find some of them aren't as small as you think. Phone calls, social media, hobbies, online, socialising – are any of these taking up more time than you realise?

One relative of mine used to wind down at the end of a day's work playing computer games for a bit. Only when his marriage started to suffer was he forced to look at how he spent his evenings and realised he was in front of a screen for about three hours a night. Impressively, he went cold turkey and stopped gaming entirely. Since then he's built a kitchen, started a vegetable garden, and still has way more time to relax with his partner of an evening.

One of the potential problems is the time at the beginning and end of activities. Going for an hour's run will entail getting changed for it and filling your water bottle, for example, and then showering and changing back afterwards. That's a lot more than an hour. Do you know how much more? So time the dog walking from when you stop the previous activity until when you start the next one – not just the time you and the dog are out of the house.

You can't hope to organise your time better in future if you don't really know how you're organising it now. Once you've done your time audit, make it a habit in future when you pick up new activities or habits to do a quick check to see how long they really take. That way you can adapt them from the start if necessary – we'll look at how to do that next.

> # GOD KNOWS A 45-MINUTE WORK MEETING CAN TAKE MORE THAN 45 MINUTES

Streamline

Now you've recognised where all your time is going, you can look at how to spend it more efficiently. We'll come on to salvaging things when you're desperately overloaded later. At the moment we're just looking at universal principles for anyone with a busy life. If you're on top of this, you should never need to deal with a crippling overload. If you are already overloaded, this is where you're aiming to get back to, so life is enjoyable again.

The first thing is to identify anything that is taking more time than it should. Like my relative and his computer gaming, are you surprised by anything? Are you spending way more time in meetings than you thought, or a bigger chunk of your evening on social media? Does your quick daily run actually take over an hour every night? Do you spend hours every day in front of the TV? Does it take until lunchtime to clear your morning emails?

Pretty much all these things can be addressed. Sometimes, just realising the extent of a time-eater is enough to shock you into reducing it. Or you can determine that you won't get sidetracked by anything at work until you've cleared all the urgent emails. If your boss expects you to attend all those meetings, talk to them. Point out what percentage of your time it takes, and what that represents in terms of your salary, and put forward some practical suggestions for using the company's time and money more effectively, and freeing you up to be more productive. Point out how much more fruitfully you could be spending those hours.

When something eats up time in getting started or finished, think about streamlining it. If your regular shop takes 40 minutes in the store, but another 40 minutes getting there and back, and unpacking the shopping, could you do it less frequently? Two shops a week instead of three will save you one of those 40 minutes. Of course, if your evening run adds 30 mins in getting changed and showered, I'm not suggesting you do a seven-hour run once a week – I'm no runner but I'm guessing that's not advisable. However, you could run for a bit longer and reduce the frequency or maybe pick up the shopping on the way home to save time there.

Most of the time, we don't think about these things. If you're happy with your work/life/relax balance, why would you? However, when things start to go wrong, you need to be pro-active about how you divvy up your time or you end up on a treadwheel where you lose sight of the things that matter in the rush to do everything you've piled into your diary, either through choice or necessity. As with getting your finances on track, consciously thinking about the things you're used to doing blindly is half the battle.

Once you have the information about where your time goes, and you take a good look at it, a lot of the solutions will be so obvious you'll wonder why it took you so long to think of them. Ironically, it's when the way you use your time matters most that you have the least time to focus on it. It might seem counter-intuitive to add this process into your week when you're already so pushed but, trust me, this is when it really needs doing.

> ## SOMETIMES, JUST REALISING THE EXTENT OF A TIME-EATER IS ENOUGH TO SHOCK YOU INTO REDUCING IT

Rate it

We know that some activities will have to go – if not now, then as soon as things get too busy. Maybe when you get that promotion, or once your parents come to live with you, or if you get serious about building that extension yourself, or get elected chair of your local sports club. Whether you're already too busy, or can just see overload heading down the road towards you, something will have to go. How much easier if you already know what that is before it happens. What's more, you can prepare other people: 'I'd love to have a regular night out, but I might have to stop if my parents move in', or 'I'd be happy to run a stall at this year's fair, but if work picks up I won't be able to do it again next year'. I'm not just thinking about the other people here, you understand. I'm thinking how much easier it will be for you to say no when you've already primed them that your involvement might be temporary.

OK, some things have to go to make room for others. But which things? Think about the things that occupy your time, and prioritise them. There are two broad categories here: things you enjoy doing, and things you need to do. Of course some things tick both boxes, such as putting the kids to bed.* That's fine – no need to get bogged down in the process. What matters is arriving at a point where you know what you'll give up if you need to – or now if you're already struggling. If you couldn't cope, would you give up book club or going to the gym? Would you leave work an hour later or catch up at home over the weekend? No need to draw up an exhaustive list – although if you'd like to, be my guest – but be clear in your own mind. If you love gardening or football or going to choir above all else, put this top of your list and know that you'd give up half a dozen other activities before this.

Equally, recognise which things you genuinely can't give up. Work, getting the kids to school, looking after your disabled sister,

---

* On a good night

feeding the family. There might be ways to speed some of these up, but essentially they're not negotiable.

This is another of those processes you can go through deliberately this time, but in future you might well get away with monitoring as you go. Whenever you say yes to a long-term commitment, think about whether you need to add a caveat that it might not be forever. When you take on a new responsibility, be clear in your own mind what will have to give if it starts to become too much.

And priorities change, of course. Right now, you might think you know what you'd give up if you needed to clear space for other things. But six months or a year from now, that could change. It's helpful to clock these things in your own mind: 'Actually, I'm enjoying this so much that when work picks up in the new year, I think I'd rather give up book club', or 'I was thinking I could see Ali less often if necessary, but given what they've been going through lately I'd definitely give them higher priority for the next few months'.

This process barely needs to be conscious when your life is going successfully and things are in balance, but it's still useful to have it bubbling in the back of your mind ready in case something suddenly upsets that balance. And the important thing is that it readies you for the fact that when new commitments arrive, some of the old will have to go.

> # THINK ABOUT THE THINGS THAT OCCUPY YOUR TIME, AND PRIORITISE THEM

RULE 27

No one is that busy

Sometimes it seems almost fashionable to be excessively busy, like a competition to see who can be most indispensable. Rule 24 was about the various reasons for this but, let me tell you, in the western world just about nobody needs to be that busy. It's a choice, and I know almost no one who couldn't free up time if they chose to. The things that keep us busy are largely luxuries that some people would be grateful to have the chance to do.

One of my friends discovered this in the worst possible way some years ago, when she was widowed very suddenly. She had three young children, and ran a business with her partner. So when he died, she had to keep the business going because it was the family's income too, which meant she was doing two people's work and had suddenly become a single parent as well. It took her a couple of years to sell the company and switch to a job that gave her a bit more time – she was conscious that her kids, having lost one parent, needed her around as much as possible.

She told me that she'd been just as busy at times before – after all, there are only 24 hours a day and there were lots of things she'd enjoyed doing. But when this crisis hit she was amazed how many things turned out to be optional when there was just no time to spare. She stopped socialising, gave up her hobbies, didn't watch TV, didn't buy any new clothes because she had no time to shop for them. In fact, she switched to online grocery shopping because there was no time to go to the supermarket. The thing that struck me most was that she told me she actually stopped biting her nails for the first time in her life – unintentionally – because there wasn't time. Her hands were constantly busy.

Her point, and mine, was that however much we might moan about being busy, it's our choice to own a dog, have a garden, go to the gym, socialise, read, watch TV, join clubs, play sport. It's also our choice to do the job we do – there's always the option of less demanding work. If we're not enjoying it, we can stop. If we are enjoying it, we shouldn't complain about being busy.

If you're genuinely overwhelmed, and you absolutely have my sympathy if that's the case, it can help to recognise just how much of what we do is a choice. Of course we don't want to give up things we enjoy, or have to say no to people, or see less of our friends. And as my friend discovered, one or two things are genuinely sacrosanct: the kids, and keeping a roof over the family's head. Those were pretty much the only non-negotiables.

She also found that it didn't last for ever. Once she managed to reorganise her life, she was able to fit some things back in again. Being a single parent doesn't leave anyone with a lot of time on their hands, but that mad rush to keep on top of the absolute basics didn't last forever, once she chose to change her work. Slowly she was able to clear some time for friends, or to read a book, or just chill in front of the TV at the end of a long day. What she tells me she really learnt, though, was to be grateful for every one of those little luxuries, to appreciate the ability to choose them and never to complain again about being too busy.

RECOGNISE JUST HOW MUCH
OF WHAT WE DO IS A CHOICE

Don't panic

Right, I promised to help if you're already at the stage where your to-do list is so long you can't see the end of it. Perhaps work is going swimmingly but you're stressfully overloaded at home. Or the other way round. Typically though, when you're overwhelmed, you're overwhelmed everywhere. One of the reasons for that is that some people are just more susceptible to it than others. If you're driven to take on too much, you'll do it across the whole of your life. So if you want to know whether this state of affairs is down to you, or due to outside forces piling tasks on you against your will, one of the best indicators is whether this is happening at home and at work. Also, is this unusual for you, or is it a fairly common occurrence?

Now listen carefully. I can give you some Rules that will help you for now but, if this is your normal MO, it will go on happening until you properly learn the rest of the Rules in this section. Understand? Now I've told you, you have only yourself to blame if you end up right back here in a couple of months' time. We can get you back on track now, but it's down to you to stay on track now you have the wherewithal. I'm not blaming you – I'm trying to help you. Not all of us are born organised, realistic, able to say no, good at making decisions. It's not easy for everyone. But if you want your life to be clearer and smoother and more streamlined and altogether more successful – which is why we're here – you have to take responsibility for making it so.

That means that as well as getting your head back above the water, you need to make sure you find strategies that will keep you afloat, and you need to use them. Won't that be great? Not only are you going to clear this overload, but it's never going to happen again. And even if it did, you'd be equipped to see it coming, and to nip it in the bud.

Countless people before you have faced a mountain of tasks and demands from work, home, kids, partner, family and beyond, and have dealt with it. And so can you. So your first task is to believe it can be done. If you go into this thinking it's impossible, you'll prove yourself right by giving up before you've made any real headway. To paraphrase Henry Ford, whether you believe you can, or whether you believe you can't, you'll be right.

So don't panic, just see this as a challenge you can get your teeth into. A few days from now everything will be back in order, and think how you'll feel then. I mean it – think about how good it's going to feel when everything is sorted. That should help motivate you. Not only will it all be sorted, but you'll have plenty of time to read and absorb all the other Rules you'll need to make sure it stays that way. You're as good as anyone else and, if they can be organised and on top of their workload, so can you.

> ## YOUR FIRST TASK IS TO BELIEVE IT CAN BE DONE

Make time

'Ha! *Make time?* Are you winding me up?' No I'm not. The way to clear an overload is to generate more time. You have to loosen a knot before you can untangle it. So the first thing to do is to create a space – a time space – in which you can address all the demands on your time. Yes, I know you have work deadlines looming, and kids to collect from school, and a wedding to go to at the weekend, and your accounts to do. But if you want to sort out this mess, you have to have a space to do it in.

For some people, making this time isn't really the problem. The challenge is to recognise the need to do it, in the midst of this mess of other things that need doing. But think about it. If you had to clear a whole room full of clutter, you'd need to make enough space to get in through the door and start dealing with it. This is exactly the same but with time instead of space.

Right. You have to stop doing some things in order to clear space to get back on top of everything else. Imagine you're a gardener (you might not have to imagine it). You have a flowerbed that's become completely overgrown. There are a few plants you like still left in it, but mostly it's full of weeds and brambles which are all spreading. Ground elder and bindweed and thistles. Nightmare. There's only one way to deal with a bed like that, as any gardener* will tell you. You have to take absolutely everything out, dispose of the weeds and clear the soil of stray roots that might reshoot, and then put the plants you actually wanted back in to the soil.

In other words, when it comes to sorting out your time and your headspace, there are things you need to get rid of completely, and other things you will have to remove from the equation and put back later. In the long term, the weeds have to go. For good. But even the roses and the delphiniums and the lilies have to come out for a little while, just so you can deal with the mess.

* Or my wife

Find someone else to walk the dog for a few days, give up your lunch breaks for the week, stop going to football practice for the rest of the month, stay an extra hour at work instead of going for an evening run, ask a friend to have the kids after school a couple of evenings, don't audition for the next am-dram production. You'll have to judge – realistically – how much time you're going to need, and then find ways to liberate it for now. Don't underestimate because, if you don't properly deal with the overload, you'll end up back where you started. But remind yourself that as soon as you're back on an even keel, you can pick all those things up again and, this time, enjoy them properly.

> YOU HAVE TO LOOSEN
> A KNOT BEFORE YOU CAN
> UNTANGLE IT

Be drastic

I once phoned someone for work to ask if he'd received my email. He replied, 'No. I've just been on holiday and I came back to 400 emails. So I deleted my inbox.' This sounded terrifying and I said, 'How can you be sure none of them were important?' His reply was 'They might have been. But if they were, people will get back to me. You just did.'

I have mixed feelings about this. Part of me thinks I'd lie awake worrying that something was more important to me than to the sender, and now I'd deleted it I couldn't be sure they'd come back to me again. On the other hand, I can absolutely see how liberating and freeing it would be just to delete your inbox.

I've no idea where you stand on this, and maybe like this guy you'd be comfortable with it. Or hate it. Or maybe you'd get fired for it. It depends on your work and on your confidence in humanity to let you know if you've missed something vital. What is unquestionable, however, is the beneficial effect it must have had on his workload. Four hundred emails he didn't have to look at, let alone deal with. That must have saved him hours of work.

Mind you, it doesn't have to be your emails. Anything that saves you time will, logically, save you more time if you do it on a bigger scale. Sometimes it's worth throwing the baby away with the bathwater.* Suppose you need to clear some space to deal with all this overwhelming, stressful stuff, and you're due to go away for the weekend. You could leave a bit later, or come back earlier on Sunday. But if you cancel the whole weekend . . . suddenly you have way more time to get back on top of things.

You've looked at how you spend your time, and maybe there are big time-wasters in there. I mean, things you might enjoy if you had the leisure to do them, but maybe you'd prefer the feeling

---

* I wish to make it transparently clear that I do not mean this literally

of calm and sanity that would come from abandoning them, at least for now. Home projects are a good example – restoring your car, or building an extension, or revamping the garden. If you ditch these – at least for the moment – you might feel even more liberated than if you deleted your inbox. After all, the emails will start coming back in again immediately, but you can hold off your project indefinitely. Of course, you might have had precious little time for it anyway, but it will have been eating at you that you needed to get on with it. The psychological effect of consciously dumping it, at least for the foreseeable, will be a huge plus.

Suppose you have to clear out a cupboard or wardrobe or room (there's a whole section on 'stuff' later on). This can take ages but, if you're moving house, or the decorators are booked for next week, or your son is moving back home, it has to be done. The drastic approach would be to throw out whole shelves or cupboards of stuff without going through them. Or of course cancel the decorators.

SOMETIMES IT'S WORTH THROWING THE BABY AWAY WITH THE BATHWATER

Switch off

Here's a Rule that will make a huge difference when it comes to finding time to sort out your head and your workload. And what's more, you'll probably find that if you keep following it once things are sorted, it will help them stay that way. Nice and simple too – just stay off the internet. Social media, rabbit holes, gaming, messaging. What's your problem?

Barely a day goes by when there isn't a news article or a magazine feature or a documentary about people who have given up their phones for a week or a month. Every single time they report that they feel much better for it, and their lives run more smoothly. And yet, even though we believe them, we struggle to do it ourselves. We know it helps, so why aren't we following suit?

That's not a rhetorical question. I'm actually asking you – why aren't you giving up your phone? You need to know the answer to this, because your phone or tablet or PC is a huge part of why you're feeling the pressure right now. Have you monitored how much of your time it occupies? If you have nothing more important to do, that's fine. But if you're buckling under the weight of your to-do list, it makes no sense.

And it's not just the time it takes. It's the fact that you're not in control of your phone. It takes nerves of steel not to look at it when it pings, not to check your socials, not to answer when it rings.* Have you considered the psychological effect of that – especially if you're already overloaded and overwhelmed? You feel your time isn't your own because you're at everyone else's beck and call.

If it was all bad, of course you'd switch off. But there are reasons to stay connected. I'm old enough to remember when you couldn't message or email. The quickest method of communication was to

---

* Yes, I know, if you're under 30 you wouldn't answer it anyway

phone, and if someone was out you had to keep trying until they answered. They might have nipped out for five minutes, or they might have gone on holiday. No way of knowing.

Modern technology is way more efficient and speeds up all sorts of transactions. Although it does make you feel you have to go at the same speed, and that doesn't always help. It also makes you anxious you're missing out, or will be forgotten, if you don't respond the moment it bleeps or pings or rings or buzzes.

So: switch off – for as long as you can manage. Maybe don't switch on in the morning until you've been up for an hour. Or put your phone into airplane mode during meal times. Or switch off for a couple of hours when you get home in the evening. If you have kids, agree some ground rules the whole family can follow. There's always some kind of option for urgent numbers to get through – so your phone knows to let your kids or your mum through even in 'do not disturb' mode.

You should find this both liberating and relaxing. If it makes you feel edgy, just do it for ten minutes to start with and build up from there. It will buy you time to sort things out for now, and if you have any sense you'll continue with it in some form. Whether that's an hour of peace every morning, or whether you can manage to turn everything on for only a couple of hours each day and enjoy even more calm time when you're in control and not your technology.

> **YOUR PHONE OR TABLET OR PC IS A HUGE PART OF WHY YOU'RE FEELING THE PRESSURE RIGHT NOW**

Get into groups

Good. We've cleared some time to get this done, and we've removed the biggest distraction – technology – for long enough to make some headway. With any luck you've also made the odd drastic decision and cleared some headspace there along with reducing the load. So you're in the starting blocks, ready to tackle this long scary list of tasks and jobs. Now what?

Let's think for a minute. You see, rushing at your list as soon as you have a spare five minutes isn't actually the best way to deal with it. Thinking might seem like a waste of time but, trust me, it speeds everything up in the long run. And if you have done your thinking and preparation properly, next time you have a spare five minutes, you'll know what's the best way to use it.

If you organise your work logically before you begin, not only will you be able to do it more efficiently, it will also look more manageable. And that has a huge psychological effect in reducing your anxiety and your stress. Instead of a whole mass of jobs, big and small, buzzing around you, the tasks will be lined up in orderly fashion waiting to be ticked off your list. You'll feel so much better before you've even done any of them.

How to organise them? The first thing to do is to get everything written down – if you do this in some kind of electronic document it will be easier to move things around, but paper is fine if you prefer. You'll probably forget the odd thing – it doesn't matter, you can just add it in when it comes to mind. Having everything written down is helpful in itself, because you remove the pressure of having to remember it. To begin with, this list might be completely random, big tasks or small, work and home. You might have jotted down 'find a new flat' next to 'drop next door's key back' or 'write up meeting notes'.

Well, clearly that's not how you want the list organised. So let's put everything into more logical groups. You're aiming for plenty of small groups of tasks – after all, you've already got one large group and it's not hugely helpful. However, if the easiest way to get there is to sort into three or four groups before you break those down further, it doesn't matter. It will just take a bit longer, but the end result will be the same. It's really down to how your own mind works and what is comfortable for you.

You are aiming to group things logically, so for work your groups might be, for example, anything relating to next month's presentation, paperwork you need to deal with, everything to do with the job vacancy you have advertised, and so on. At home your lists might be stuff to do with the school PTA committee, things to buy/sort out for your holiday, stuff that needs mending, and so on.

Well done. You're well on your way now and, crucially, you can literally see what needs to be done. Time to move on to the next stage.

> # YOU'RE AIMING FOR PLENTY OF SMALL GROUPS OF TASKS

Prioritise

You have a clear list of tasks, conveniently organised into manageable groups. No, you can't start doing them yet. I mean, which ones would you start with? You don't know, do you? So the next job is to put the groups into some kind of order that tells you how to work through them. In other words, you need to prioritise.

There are two different ways you can prioritise tasks (or groups of tasks). You could do the most urgent things first. Or the most important – which isn't at all the same thing. If you're a sales manager, organising next summer's sales conference has got to be high on your priority list for importance. On the other hand, if this is only October, it can't be that urgent. A couple of days dealing with other things won't matter.

It's a big help that you've sorted everything into groups, as you should be able to see now. Give or take the occasional very urgent job, you only have to prioritise a few groups, not hundreds of different tasks. Right, let's start with three categories of groups. A section for groups that are urgent, a section for the important ones and – because you're going to need this – a section for those that are both urgent *and* important.

Are things starting to feel a bit clearer? It should be obvious that the first thing to do is deal with the things in that final category – the ones that are both urgent and important. Follow that with the ones that are urgent but not particularly important, bearing in mind that they don't warrant having a lot of time spent on them. It might be that just a quick holding email or a message will tick them off the list – or at least move them into a non-urgent group.

Now look at this. Sit back for a minute and take in the view. You've been panicky and anxious because there's so much to do. You were feeling overwhelmed. But let's see where we are now:

- You have a list of things that need doing so you can stop carrying it round in your head. You can add things to this list any time you need to without them having to clutter up your brain on the way.

- You've organised this list into useful groups so you can see where you are and deal with things as efficiently as possible.

- You have some time to spare because you've used every trick in the book* to liberate the space you need to deal with all this.

- You have done all the urgent things you had to do.

So now you're left with a whole load of non-urgent tasks. This is likely to be the bulk of your to-do list but, hold on, they're non-urgent. Whoopee! Now you can use the time you've created to work through these, roughly in order of importance. If the odd urgent thing comes in while you're dealing with them, you'll have the time and headspace to do something about it. Anything non-urgent that arrives in your in-tray just gets added to the relevant group and dealt with when its turn comes round.

So long as you've followed all the Rules that stop the same backlog building up again, you're already back in control and looking ahead to a relaxed, streamlined lifestyle once you've just ticked off these last few groups of tasks. Phew!

SIT BACK FOR A MINUTE AND TAKE IN THE VIEW

---

* Yep, this one

Get smart

When you're trying to work through an overload of tasks – and when you're making sure you keep on top of things next time – you need to come up with smart strategies to streamline the process. I'll give you a couple of examples and then you can think up your own. Or pick the brains of the people you know who are already effortlessly efficient and successful.

So here's my first strategy: have an email system that makes your life easier. For a start, use your email archive properly, making sure you have folders and sub-folders for everything to make it really easy to file – and find – anything. OK, as soon as something is dealt with, you now know where to archive it. That means the only emails in your inbox or your sent items should be ones that still need action. Your inbox is your in-tray, your to-do list – everything in it requires action from you, so make sure it contains as little as possible and stay on top of it. Archive everything as soon as you've dealt with it.

Go through your inbox at the end (or beginning) of every day, and clear out anything that isn't waiting to be actioned. At the same time, go through your sent items. This is really important. You know how frustrating it is when you leave the ball in someone else's court and they don't get back to you? It makes it so easy for you to take your eye off the ball – it's not in your court after all – and next thing some deadline is looming and you realise you never heard back. So everything in your sent items gets archived *except* if it's waiting on a response. Since you're going through it daily, you'll be well aware that this person or that hasn't replied, so you can chase them in good time. Archiving everything else routinely should mean there are relatively few emails at any one time awaiting a reply, and you'll have a clear eye on them.

With this system – or you might devise your own equivalent that achieves the same ends (thinking for yourself is positively encouraged) – your email system is making your life much easier and more streamlined, and making sure things happen when they should. All you have to do is keep on top of it in lots of quick easy bursts.

I said I'd give you another strategy, so here it is. Get other people to do some of your tasks for you. Delegate, in a sense. If you earn enough, you can pay people – to clean your house, mow your lawn, wash your car, do your accounts, cut your hair. Think about this logic: if you earn for the sake of argument £40 an hour, and you can pay someone to mow the grass for £20 an hour, it makes more sense to work while they mow than to stop work to cut the grass.

And what if, like many people, you can't afford it? Very often you can find ways to barter. One friend of mine had a small building company. They didn't find writing easy so I wrote press releases and leaflets for them, and they fixed odd things round the house for me. Looking after four or five children isn't much harder than looking after just a couple. So why not mind a friend's kids alongside your own to give your friend an afternoon free, and they can return the favour for you. That might be a one-off, or a permanent arrangement.

See? There are lots of ways to free up time, and streamline your work or your home admin, so you can stay calmly in charge of your life with plenty of time to give to the things that matter to your success.

COME UP WITH SMART STRATEGIES TO STREAMLINE THE PROCESS

Edit in big chunks

When you have too much to do, you need to do less. It's not rocket science. You know how much is 'too much' – it's the point where it gets in the way of achieving what you want to. Maybe you can't succeed at work because your home life is taking up too much of your time, perhaps you don't get enough time with the kids because you're working too hard, maybe you can't make as much money as you'd like because you have to spend three days a week caring for your relatives, maybe you're permanently exhausted because you rarely get time to sleep properly, perhaps you spend so much time making your boat seaworthy that you never have time to sail it.*

The first thing to do is to recognise that this is unsustainable, and something has to change. Maybe this will be permanent if you don't take action, or maybe it's finite but the end is further away than you can cope with – for example, you know things will change for the better next year, but it's only February and you're not going to make it that far without some let up in the pressure.

It's all very well getting back in control of your emails or finding an hour to do your accounts. Those things may clear your to-do list backlog, but they won't stop it building straight back up again. If you're prone to being overwhelmed, you need to make some bigger decisions to stop it happening again and again.

As a writer, I know that if I write something that has to be 50,000 words long and it turns out to be a couple of hundred words over, I can go through it and take out a word here or a sentence there to get it down to length. But if it's several thousand words over, I have to edit out whole chunks and chapters. Tidying up the odd phrase isn't going to cut it.

---

* That is both a thing and a metaphor. I speak from experience in both cases

Life is just the same. If you're having a bit of a busy week, you can come into work a bit early, or cancel your night out on Friday, and get yourself back on track. But if you're consistently stressed and unable to cope under the pressure, some things will have to be edited out completely.

So once you've cleared a bit of thinking space, use it to work out which permanent changes you'll make. Remember how we audited where our time goes earlier? And rated activities according to how much we needed or wanted to do them? Now is the time to use this process and decide what you have to give up. I know you enjoy some of these things, but you don't enjoy the collective pressure they put on your time. It may well be a wrench to stop going to football, or step down as union rep, but look at what you get back in return – time, peace, relaxation, sanity.

> ## SOME THINGS WILL HAVE TO BE EDITED OUT COMPLETELY

Don't fill in the blanks

A stitch in time . . . literally. If you're really struggling to cope with the pressure on your day at the moment, the last few Rules are going to help you. Even so, you need to learn this Rule or you could solve the problem now, ease the pressure, and then find yourself right back here in a few months' or years' time. Then again, if you're only starting to feel the strain but are still coping, now is absolutely the time to take action so things don't get on top of you.

Many of us are inclined to take on more than we can cope with, for reasons like the ones in Rule 35, and I suppose because we think we'll cope until we discover we were wrong. OK, these Rules will help this time, but wouldn't it be lovely if there wasn't a next time? If this was the last time you'd ever have to feel this way for more than a few days?

The key to that is all about self-awareness. Look, it's inarguable: if you take on more without giving anything up, the pressure will increase. Every time. So you have to know your limits. It's different for everyone, but we all have only 24 hours in a day. What's more, things will intrude on your time that you hadn't planned for – they always do – so if you have no leeway in the system you're going to struggle when that happens.

Maybe a relative is ill and needs looking after, or maybe you have to plan a friend's party, or step in at work for an absent colleague. Some of these things might be fun, but they'll still take up time. And just because you and I can't predict which of them will happen and when, we can still confidently predict that some of them will happen. Your friend's party might be fun to plan and only take a few days, and you'll be happy to put in the extra time. But your relative might be ill for months and need a meal cooked for them every day – you want to help but that's a big knock-on effect on the rest of your week. If you had no leeway before they fell ill, how are you going to be coping a couple of months in?

So once you've got yourself to the point where you're happy with your work/life balance, you're happily occupied but not overloaded, you have the time to invest in whatever area of your life you want to . . . keep it that way. Don't take on anything extra unless you give something up. Recognise that keeping this balance, with a little bit of room for manoeuvre, is the sweet spot you're aiming for. As soon as you start to feel even a little bit too pressured, take action. Think about what's causing it. Unless it's very short term, and you're sure you're happy to put in the extra time for a short period, now is the time to tweak things and steady the boat. Don't wait for the storm to hit.

Once you get good at this, you'll learn to anticipate. You should be aware that starting a family, for example, will take up a load of time and other things will need to make way. However that might also be true of a promotion or a change of job. Or a change of living arrangements, or a new hobby. It doesn't hurt to know at the back of your mind what you'll give up if the pressure starts to build – trips to the gym, chairing a local committee, D&D evenings. With the right attitude and a bit of forethought, time overload should be a thing of the past.

> # IF YOU TAKE ON MORE WITHOUT GIVING ANYTHING UP, THE PRESSURE WILL INCREASE

EMOTIONS

This book is all about creating success by being in control of key aspects of your life, and high on that list for many people is their own emotions. When you're feeling happy, positive and confident, there's nothing in life you can't achieve. Think of all the things you can do when you're not scared, all the friends or jobs you have when you're confident, all the activities you really enjoy when anxiety doesn't get in the way.

We all of us have times when we're able to steel ourselves and tackle things despite our fears, worries, doubts, anxieties. But even the most adept Rules Player sometimes shies away from doing a thing we'd like to be able to master. We all draw those lines in different places, and indeed you and I and everyone else will do a thing one day that we struggle to do the next.

Of course that's normal, but it doesn't make it helpful. Wouldn't you like to apply for that exciting job even when it feels scary? Or go to that party despite the fact you won't know many people? Or commit to this relationship – or walk away from it – despite your past experiences?

Of course these things interact with each other, and feeling overwhelmed in one area of your life can make it harder to find the confidence, enthusiasm and drive you need to achieve what you want in other areas. Your emotions can get between you and your ability to succeed, and add to the pressure and the sense of overload.

That's where these next few Rules can help. They're not a magic wand, but understanding how your emotions might be holding you back can be a big part of getting on top of them.

Know yourself

If you're serious about stopping your emotions getting in the way of your life, the first thing you need to do is to recognise where and when you're holding yourself back. I must stress, for this and the following Rules, that I'm not a qualified psychotherapist and I've never met you personally, so I'm not presuming to treat you for serious mental health conditions, or any kind of PTSD or history of trauma. This is about those day-to-day character traits that are holding you back.

So what are they? They may not be flaws in themselves, morally speaking. They may simply be aspects of your personality that prevent you from doing the things you need to do. Being shy around other people, for example, can often make you likeable. However it can also get in the way of doing things that call for confidence.

Before you can address these traits, you need to know what they are. Fingers crossed lack of self-awareness isn't one of them, because that's the quality you need here. The idea is not to beat yourself up – even if you identify low self-esteem as one of them – but consciously to know the areas you want to work on. We're focusing on how you can be as successful as you'd like, so this isn't about dealing with everything you've ever wished you could change about yourself. It's about recognising what changes would directly influence your success.

Suppose you'd like to progress faster in your career. Depending on the work you do, the thing that's holding you back might be lack of confidence, or being prone to becoming too stressed to work effectively, or shyness. So that's where you need to focus. Perhaps work is going fine but you struggle with family relationships, and that's really important to you. So what's holding you back here – anxiety? Or is your tendency to become angry making it hard to stay on good terms with family when you have disagreements?

Or are you not assertive enough about what you need from the relationship?

Perhaps success for you is about money or status. Are you impulsive about spending money that you'd do better to save and/or invest? Do people not take you as seriously as you'd like – in which case what can you work on to change that?

You're not looking for a list of ways to turn yourself into a different person. You just need to see where to focus your efforts to make the biggest difference in the areas that matter most to you. You'll still be you, in all your wonderfulness – only a bit more assertive, or calmer, or better able to talk in front of a group of people, or to deal with a stressful week.

I'm going to look at some of the more common traits that can interfere in your life-plan over the next few Rules and give you a starting point for getting to grips with them.

RECOGNISE WHERE YOU'RE HOLDING YOURSELF BACK

Know where you flourish

Before you even start work on the emotions that you feel are getting in your way, I want you to stop for a minute and think about your strengths. For one thing, it's always good for your self-esteem to remind yourself of the qualities you can be happy with. It's also a reminder that while we all have flaws, we also all have good points.

In terms of your success, it helps to be aware of your strengths so you can play to them. Perhaps you struggle a bit with stress at work, but you're great with people. Remember that – and make sure you take every opportunity that it gives you to shine. That will get you noticed when it matters and help to cement people's positive view of you despite the occasional stressy moment.

However, if you drill down, you find that even in the areas where you think you're lacking, you still have strengths. I know plenty of people who consider themselves under-assertive but who have no difficulty asserting themselves with their kids. So clearly they have the skills – they just need to learn to apply them more widely.

One of my kids is about the calmest, most chilled person I've ever met. Always good in a crisis, never panics and laid back about everything. Except admin. Give him a form to fill in and he freezes in terror or starts to get really snappy and snarky. Clearly he's capable of taking things in his stride so he doesn't need to learn a whole new way of being. He just needs to work out why he gets triggered by admin and how to use the skills he already has on those occasions when he's presented with paperwork. Of course, if he could live a successful life without ever encountering a form, he wouldn't need to address it at all. That's quite tricky though.

Maybe he needs to get to the point where he can afford a PA to do his paperwork. Interestingly he has a sister who gets very anxious doing her own admin, but is particularly good with other people's because she doesn't have anything personally at stake.

She helps her brother, but it's also a reminder that actually she doesn't struggle with paperwork – it's just her anxiety that gets in the way. So admin is actually one of her strengths, even when it feels like shaky ground.

I've known people who could confidently stand up and give a talk in front of a roomful of people at work, but were hugely anxious about giving a wedding speech. And plenty of people who are prone to anger when they're stressed, but are the picture of calm diplomacy when things are going well.

When you think about it, very few people are permanently anxious, or never confident, or shy in any situation. And that will apply to you too. Whatever the Achilles heel that holds you back, there will be times it's not a problem or circumstances where you excel regardless. Not only should that boost your belief that you can do this, it will also help you find the skills you need to draw on.

> # STOP FOR A MINUTE AND THINK ABOUT YOUR STRENGTHS

Keep a lid on anxiety

If you know you're prone to worry or feel anxious, you'll likely know when it's going to happen. Meeting new people, heights, speaking in public, flying, interviews, spiders, tricky conversations.* Most likely you don't feel anxious in all these situations, so remind yourself you're quite capable of not being anxious, even when other people might be. You can do this.

One of the typical responses to anxiety is to imagine in your head what might go wrong. You might drop your notes, the plane might crash, you might be asked a question you can't answer, the spider might refuse to negotiate. But listen, except maybe with the spider, you must realise that these are not likely, even if they're possible. You probably won't drop your notes, so why are you so worried about it? If you really *believed* the plane was going to crash, why did you buy a ticket?

When you catch yourself thinking like this, make yourself imagine the best case scenario instead of the worst one. It's more likely after all. Imagine the talk going well and everyone clapping, or the plane landing smoothly and safely, depositing you somewhere you want to be. These thoughts are much more realistic, and will help quell your anxiety rather than feeding it.

The other big help is to know what you're doing. Anyone might be anxious at giving a talk or attending an interview they haven't prepared for, so prepare. Rehearse. Know your stuff. Practise greeting new people and think up a couple of questions to get the conversation started. Knowing in your own mind that you're ready for this will go a long way to reducing the worry.

And if you're still worrying about that worst case scenario, have a Plan B ready. What will you do if you drop your notes? What will you say if you're asked a question you can't answer? If you've

---

* I've had some tricky conversations with spiders in my time

practised and prepared these things are unlikely, but if you have a solution anyway – or a glass and a piece of card – what's to worry about?

At times of extreme worry, anxiety can develop into feelings of panic. Maybe just before an interview, or when you feel overloaded with things to do (although once you've read the earlier section on Time that should be a thing of the past). If this is occasional and you aren't seeking professional help but just want a way to calm down, deep breathing can help. Focus on your chest and diaphragm going in and out, count slowly . . . the details aren't important. What matters is that you slow down your breathing and focus on something that isn't the cause of your worry.

To shift focus, some people try to note three things they can hear, three things they can see, and three ways they can move their body. But you could just as well try to think of ten animals beginning with B or twelve things that were on last week's shopping list. Recite poetry in your head, or do a sudoku on your phone – I'm a big fan of sudoku because the whole game is a process of putting things neatly in order, which gives you a reassuring feeling of everything being alright. Works for me anyway.

> **REMIND YOURSELF YOU'RE QUITE CAPABLE OF NOT BEING ANXIOUS**

Calm the stress

Stress and anxiety can often go together, but they're not the same thing. While anxiety is worry – often about something very unlikely – stress is a reaction to outside influences that you feel unable to cope with. In some cases stress can be long term, if the trigger for it isn't going away – a difficult relationship with your partner, debt, too much to do at work. At its worst it can cause a range of physical symptoms from illness to fatigue to insomnia, along with mood swings, irritability and depression.

It's important to recognise the early signs of stress if you can, and don't assume everything will magically come right. Take action as soon as you can, in case the magic doesn't happen. The first and most obvious action you can take is to remove the cause of the stress. Clearly there will be times this is impossible, but you'd be surprised how often there is something you can do.

This is really the crux of what all the Rules in this book are about. Remove all the barriers and impediments that make your life harder, and lo and behold things will run smoothly and your life will be a success. That's just common sense. We've already had sections on how to put things right if your finances are making you stressed, for example, or if you don't have enough time and are feeling overwhelmed with too much to do. Coming up are more Rules to help you clear the clutter – literal and metaphorical – that is putting you under too much pressure.

Obviously you're not restricted to the Rules in this book. If you know you're stressed, and you've thought through the reason, you can often do something about it. If you're consistently overworked, go and talk to your boss. Give them chapter and verse, and they may well find a way to reduce your workload or to get you help. If your relationship is making you stressed, talk to your partner. It's always better than not talking, and sometimes things are way easier to resolve than you thought. If keeping on top of the garden is just too much with your busy lifestyle, turn most of it over to grass you can just mow, or pave it, or find someone who can help out.

There's so often a solution that reduces the stress enough to cope, even if it doesn't get rid of it altogether. And sometimes the answer is drastic – get another job, or end the relationship – well, if that makes you happier it's a good solution, isn't it? There's stress in most things in life, it's just how you see it. We call some kinds of stress challenge or stimulation and we see them as positive. So the aim isn't to remove all stress – that would make life very boring.

If you really can't eliminate, or at least reduce, the thing that's stressing you, you need to be able to cope with it. The important thing is to stave off the worst symptoms, both physical and mental, so those are the areas to focus on. To stay healthy and retain the energy you need, make sure you're eating well, exercising enough, and sleeping properly. These can be the first things to go when you're stressed, but they're the defence mechanisms you most need to stay in good health. For your mental wellbeing, take time to do whatever relaxes you – go for walks, meditate, garden, video game, collect stamps, just chill. And make sure you have supportive people around you who will listen, help, take you out of yourself, and make you laugh.

> # DON'T ASSUME EVERYTHING WILL MAGICALLY COME RIGHT

Stay cool

Most of us who have short tempers are that way for a reason. Maybe some people just come in to the world that way but quite a lot of us, and yes I am including myself here, have other reasons too. In my case, I was on the receiving end of quite a bit of anger as a child. It doesn't excuse dishing it out to other people, but it helps me understand it, and that's part of learning to master it.

Anyone can get irritable from time to time, and once in a while anger might be entirely justified – setting aside the question of how you express it. However, if you're prone to get angry about things that others take in their stride, or to fly off the handle easily, or to take your frustration out on other people, that's not good. It's not good for the other people, and it's not good for you.

Being angry is bad for your health for a start – not the odd rare burst, but as a common occurrence it puts your system under stress. It's also not an enjoyable emotion. No one wants to keep feeling angry, and it's particularly unpleasant if you feel you're not fully in control of your behaviour. Even when you trust yourself not to be violent or abusive, you may still be intimidating other people and unable to stop.

And then there's the effect on your life. People who often get angry damage their relationships, at work and at home. People will feel intimidated, or reluctant to express their views, or simply avoid being around you in situations that might provoke you. Anger can damage your career, your relationship and your friendships.

I'm far from perfect, and I'm certainly not going to hold myself up as a brilliant example to follow, but I have managed to become a much less angry person than I once was because I recognised that I was suffering more than anyone else. Yes, of course I'm still a grumpy old sod quite a lot of the time, but I don't shout at people any more. I don't actually want to be someone who shouts and gets angry, so I've stopped.

It's not easy, and I have the occasional relapse, but the biggest breakthrough for me was recognising when something was going to get me angry *before* it actually happened, and just walking away. Letting go, backing down, avoiding the triggers that would tip me over to the point I couldn't hold back.

The other thing that helps me hugely is finding the humour in a situation. It's very hard to get angry when you're enjoying the funny side. I would frequently get snappy and angry with the phone company when they cut me off again, or the electricity supplier when they overcharged me, or a department store that refused to exchange something that was clearly faulty. Nowadays, I reflect on how to turn it into an entertaining anecdote and, the more obstructive they are, the funnier my story will be.

Look everyone has to find their own strategy for coping with anger – and some may even need professional help. The thing is to realise that your anger is interfering with your ability to enjoy life to the full, and resolve to deal with it.

IT'S NOT GOOD FOR THE OTHER PEOPLE, AND IT'S NOT GOOD FOR YOU

Raise your self-esteem

Here's another emotion that gets in your way and which often has deep roots. Again, if you're really struggling you may need a professional to help you – and that's not me. However I can report back on what I've witnessed benefiting other people, and it shouldn't be hard to lift your self-esteem on a bad day or when you're going through a shaky phase.

Self-esteem is all about recognising your own value. Acknowledging your strengths. For a lot of people it can be a bit fragile, and it gets knocked back if you can't do something as well as you think you should, or if someone makes a critical comment, or if you aren't making the progress you feel you should – in your career, as a parent, financially, or wherever.

When this happens, people who are prone to low self-esteem tend to see this as evidence that they're not good enough, smart enough, capable enough. Not everyone is given to poor self-esteem though, and there are people who can take a knock-back without seeing it as a judgement on themselves. So what can we learn from them?

The big difference for these people is that they look at things much more specifically. They don't see every failure or shortcoming as a character flaw. And in the same way, they don't see any genuine flaws as reflecting on themselves in a broader sense. Suppose two people apply for the same job, and neither gets it. The internal dialogue for them goes roughly like this . . .

- Low self-esteem: 'I knew I wouldn't get it, I'm useless at interview. They obviously thought I just wasn't good enough.'

- High self-esteem: 'That's a shame. Clearly there was another applicant better qualified than me. I should ask for feedback, in case there's something I can learn for next time.'

So one person thinks they've failed, and it's a symptom of their general lack of ability. The other thinks they were unlucky, and maybe they can learn from it. The person with low self-esteem has taken this setback as a reflection not only on their suitability for the job but on their whole character, and look how that can get in the way of success. Whereas the person with high self-esteem is using this to drive themselves forwards.

So when you encounter a situation that makes you feel bad about yourself, keep this in mind. Maybe your report for the boss didn't get the fulsome praise you'd hoped for, or one of your kids is going through a phase of behaving badly, or you can't seem to get back to your personal best in your sport, or the house is a mess and you still haven't cleaned it like you meant to. None of this makes you a different person, for better or for worse. Maybe you've been pressured for time, maybe most kids go through bad patches, maybe you need to ask for a couple of pointers for report writing, perhaps you could try a different training regime.

There are simple explanations for most mistakes, shortcomings and failures, which have nothing whatever to do with your value as a person. So look for the simple explanation, and remind yourself how well your presentation went down, or how well behaved the kids usually are, or how clean the bathroom is, or how good your personal best actually is.

> ## THERE ARE PEOPLE WHO CAN TAKE A KNOCK-BACK WITHOUT SEEING IT AS A JUDGEMENT ON THEMSELVES

Build your confidence

Since we've just been looking at self-esteem, I'm not referring to confidence in that sense here. I mean confidence in the sense of feeling able to cope with things, your belief in your ability to cope with the new job, or be a parent, or learn to drive safely, or enjoy a holiday on your own, or move to a new part of the country, or hold your own as a member of the choir.

Part of this, of course, can overlap with emotions like anxiety or your self-esteem. But confidence is about trusting yourself to be able to manage something that you don't have proof you can manage. Either you've tried before and it hasn't worked out, or you've never tried it. So you have to take it on trust you can do it. If you struggle to find this confidence, that's when you start to feel anxious.

So let's find that trust, shall we? I'll be honest, confidence tends to build as you get older because there are more things you've done before – or at least done something similar – so it's easier to find that self-belief. Mind you, I'm always saying how good it is to step out of your comfort zone at any age, and testing your confidence is one reason why.

When you're facing something you don't feel confident about, you can build up your trust in your ability by thinking about it in the right way. For a start, you can remind yourself of any support you have. If you're learning to drive, remember you're not going to be alone in the car, and there'll be an instructor or friend who knows exactly what they're doing. As a new parent, you'll have all the help and advice of all your friends and family who have been there before.* Alongside that, remind yourself how many people have learnt to drive before, or have become parents successfully. If they can do it, why wouldn't you be able to? If your new boss didn't think you were up to the job, why did they give it to you?

---

* Trust me, you'll have *significantly* more advice than you want

Another positive line of thought is to consider what similar experience you have. OK you haven't been on holiday on your own before, but maybe you've been away on your own for work, or you know you're good at making friends. This might be the first time you've looked after your own kitten, but if you grew up around cats how hard can it be?

The better prepared you are, the more confident you'll feel. So watch online videos, or study the holiday itinerary, or go to parenting classes,* or enrol on a training course. Your feeling of under-confidence can be really handy in prompting you to prepare thoroughly so you succeed when you get there.

In many cases, try asking yourself what's the worst that can happen? If you hate the holiday, don't go again. If singing in a choir isn't for you, then stop. You'll have learnt something useful about yourself, and there's usually no harm done.

And, lest I forget to encourage you to step out of your comfort zone, enjoy the frisson of trying something new. Don't label it anxiety when you could see it as excitement or adrenaline. Those butterflies in your stomach can be a good thing. How boring would life be if we only ever did things we already know we can do?

> # DON'T LABEL IT ANXIETY WHEN YOU COULD SEE IT AS EXCITEMENT

---

* For the new baby, not the kitten

Say it how it is

The problem with not being assertive enough is that there are too many times when you don't get what you want. I mean, it's not good for us to get what we want all the time, but there should be a better reason than not being able to articulate what it is. If this is a problem for you, why can't you say how you feel? Do you think you're being unreasonable? Are you afraid of the other person's reaction? Did you grow up believing it was rude or wrong to say no to people? Do you think you don't deserve it? As with so many things, understanding where you're coming from makes it so much easier to get to where you want to be.

Let's take one of the most common and problematic examples of under-assertiveness: the inability to say no. Do you find yourself agreeing to things you don't actually want, because you can't work out how to say no? We touched on this earlier as one of the big reasons why people can become overwhelmed by a towering to-do list or an overload of work. See, when you're not assertive enough, it can cause you huge problems that stop you enjoying life, or achieving what you want to.

It's completely fine to say no to things – other people do it all the time. However if you find it hard, it can help to offer something instead of a yes, as we saw in Rule 17. For example, 'I can't help, but I know someone who might' or 'I can't do it next week, but I might be able to look at it later in the month', or even 'I wish I could say yes but I just don't have the time'. If you can't think of a way to say no on the spot, you can always ask to think about it, and then go back and say no when you've come up with the right words. Try not to apologise for saying no – you have nothing to apologise for and if you keep saying sorry you send yourself a subconscious message that you are somehow at fault. That's the underlying issue we're trying to overcome.

Here's another downside of not being assertive. It can make it really hard for you to raise issues that are causing you problems.

You can't get across to your partner how much of a problem it is in the relationship that they're busy elsewhere several evenings a week, because you don't just say it straight. Or your boss doesn't realise how overworked you are, because you don't like to raise it, until some vital task slips through the gaps and now everyone's in a mess and it looks like your fault.

It really is hard when you're made this way, but you need to find a way to talk about these things before you lose your relationship or your job, or at least keep finding them a struggle. Look, other people manage to have these conversations so clearly it is OK to say it. It's just a matter of finding the words. So practise. As with saying no, imagine broaching the topic and look for ways to phrase what you need to say that don't feel rude or demanding. You should be better at this than most people.

Do be clear though. If you need more help at work, say 'I'm concerned that my workload is too big now I've taken over the Blyton project, and without some help something will fall through the cracks'. Don't say, 'Well, I was just sort of wondering, I mean I know we're all busy, but you know, the Blyton project's quite big, and of course I'm really pleased I'm working on it . . . '. If you only want to say this once, make sure you say it unequivocally.

> **IF YOU ONLY WANT TO SAY THIS ONCE, MAKE SURE YOU SAY IT UNEQUIVOCALLY**

Don't be afraid

Fear is a primeval emotion that is there to keep us safe. If you don't have any fear of predators, or dangerous terrain, you won't last long. It's an evolutionary necessity – children develop deep fears around the age of three or four. In the absence of genuine threats they'll become frightened of the dark, or monsters, or strangers, or dogs. We need to be able to be scared, so even if you feel your fears are getting in your way, it doesn't mean they're bad feelings. Just good feelings in the wrong places. You don't want to lose your fear of jumping off tall buildings or stepping into the path of speeding cars.

However, if your fear is focused on things that aren't rational and don't seem to scare everyone else, that's when they can hamper you and interfere with a happy and successful life. In the end, the answer is not to avoid the object of fear – unless it's something very obscure and easy to avoid – but to address it.

I have a friend who is scared of using the cooker in case they burn themselves. Another friend breaks out into a cold sweat at the prospect of having to speak in front of a group of people. And I know several people who start to shake and panic if they see a spider. These examples are not just anxieties that give them an unpleasant adrenaline rush, they are real fears that engender a flight or fight response. But you can't keep running away from your kitchen or taking up arms against a house spider.

This level of fear is frustrating but tolerable if you're terrified of lions, for example,* or guinea pigs. You can be fairly confident you won't encounter one unexpectedly, and you can live a happy and successful life without your fear hampering your career or your love life. But a terror of flying, or open water, or spiders will sooner or later cause problems you don't need. What if a spider

---

* As long as you don't live in Africa. Or work as a zoo keeper

runs across the boardroom table during a vital meeting? Or your kids want to go on a trip to the beach?

Look, I'm not going to cure your fear in a couple of pages. The message I want to give you from seeing other people coping – or not coping – with deep-seated fears is that the ones who face the problem are much happier than the ones who try to hide from it. I've known people get medical help, or hypnosis, or take beta blockers. And others who have just tackled the thing in small doses and built up. In the end, your brain needs to learn that these things are not the threat it thinks they are. You can start speaking in front of very small groups of people you know well and build up from there. Learn to share a room with a tiny spider to begin with. Take swimming lessons from someone with experience of teaching people like you.

And you don't have to learn to love flying or public speaking or cooking or swimming. You just want to get these quite understandable but unhelpful responses to a point where they don't interfere with the rest of your life.

> **YOUR BRAIN NEEDS TO LEARN THAT THESE THINGS ARE NOT THE THREAT IT THINKS THEY ARE**

Don't be a wallflower

One of the things that makes life tricky for shy people is that they feel they're the only one. Trust me, if you're in a roomful of people who don't all know each other well, most of them will be feeling shy to some degree. You just can't see it – as they can't with you, partly because they're too busy worrying about their own feelings. Shyness can feel very isolating and encourages you to focus in on yourself and how you're coping in the situation.

Of course, that makes you self-conscious about it, and that's a big part of why it feels so uncomfortable. Once people stop being shy, they focus on the people and activity around them instead, and they relax. Actually, you know this from those occasions when you're surrounded by family or close friends. I imagine that feels fine. Even if you're one of the quieter ones, that's just you and everyone is used to it – they probably don't think about it, and maybe they even appreciate it.

So the trick to coping with feeling shy is to focus elsewhere and stop thinking about your own feelings. So what are you going to focus on? Other people of course. People love talking about themselves, so let them do it. If you start to relax and contribute more to the conversation, that's great. If they continue to do most of the talking, that's great too. Everyone's happy.

Now all you need to do is get them to talk, so you can listen (everyone loves a good listener – they're going to like you). So you just need to ask questions. And obviously, because you worry you won't be able to think of questions in the heat of the moment, you're going to prepare the questions in advance. Before you go to any event, work or social, prepare a few questions that will be relevant to the other people there. You don't want questions with a yes or no or one-word answer, because they don't keep the conversation going, unless you have a follow-up question ready.

Suppose you're going to a big wedding. I know, scary, especially if you hardly know anyone. But if you find yourself standing next to a stranger ask them which of the wedding couple they know. That invites a one-word answer of course, but follow it up by asking how they know them. You see? That could be a whole story. Have another few questions prepared, but you may not even need them. If conversation flags at all the other person is bound to ask you the same question back. And all of that pre-supposes that they didn't start chatting to you before you ever had a chance to deploy your questions.

It's worth having a line prepared to get you out of a flagging conversation. You probably won't need it, but it's reassuring to have it in your repertoire. Suit it to the occasion but it can be as simple as excusing yourself to get a drink, go to the loo, speak to someone you've just seen, find your car keys – it's good to have a safety net.

And then enjoy! Find the interest in other people, go off-piste and ask questions you didn't prepare just because you'd like to know the answer, and before you know it you may find you're actually enjoying yourself.

> # IT'S GOOD TO HAVE A
> # SAFETY NET

RULE 47

Pick yourself up

This isn't the place to tackle clinical depression, and I'm not the man to tackle it. However many of us who are lucky enough to have sidestepped the worst of depression can still go through periods of low mood. It's frustrating for a day or two, but if it persists it can lead to a generalised inertia and an unwillingness to get on and do the things we'd like to. It can also make you feel anxious or irritable, interfere with your sleep, reduce your libido and lower your self-esteem.

If you're quite often dogged by this it can become quite a problem, so it's worth knowing how to deal with it when it starts to intrude. This seems to be becoming more prevalent, for several reasons. Scientists reckon that poor diet is a big part of it – too much processed food. If you think this might be the case for you, you know what to do. Obviously while you're feeling low and unmotivated isn't the best time to freshen up your diet – I can see that – but you can do your best for now and as soon as you feel brighter you can make a point of modifying your diet to exclude more of the processed stuff.

You don't need to be a heavy drinker for alcohol to become a factor. It may not cause you to feel down, but it can make it a lot harder to pick yourself up again. So resist the temptation to drink when you're feeling flat.

A sedentary lifestyle is another culprit so again, when you can find the motivation, get a bit more active. It may not be realistic to take up sport in a big way, but weekend walks, taking the stairs instead of the escalator, a spot of gardening, going for a swim, kicking a football around in the park with your kids, these are all small activities but if you can turn them into habits they will make a difference.

Sometimes you have a pretty good idea what's behind your lack of enthusiasm and general ennui. Low-level stress can trigger it, maybe at work, or an ongoing issue in a relationship, or family pressures. It's a useful sign that you need to resolve any of these things you can, before your mood deteriorates or you become much more stressed. So identify the underlying problem and focus your attention on dealing with it.

Simply being around other people will help you, and make sure you choose people who lift you and make you laugh. Once again, this is exactly the time when bothering to make social arrangements seems like too much effort. Being aware of this is half the battle so push yourself, even if it's just a quick coffee with someone or an evening down the pub. No need to organise a lavish party or plan a weekend away.

Another strategy that works for a lot of people is to be creative. Whether you like to write, sew, play music, paint, cook, photograph, crochet, dance, build, design . . . this might be the thing that gives you back your mojo when you're feeling low.

> MAKE SURE YOU CHOOSE
> PEOPLE WHO LIFT YOU AND
> MAKE YOU LAUGH

Don't be ashamed

Who hasn't had the odd moment of embarrassment at a stupid mistake or a thoughtless comment? At the other end of the spectrum, though, shame can be crippling. You can feel so mortified that you can't show your face, or feel you don't deserve to do well or to have what you want.

When you feel ashamed, it's a view that colours your whole sense of worth as a person. You may feel guilty about a particular action – rightly or wrongly – but shame spreads more broadly and makes you feel inadequate as a person. It can be triggered by guilt, but not necessarily. If you feel shame, you're likely to feel other people are judging you as harshly as you do yourself, or at least they would be if they knew what you know.

It should be clear that strong feelings of shame can really get in the way of your hopes and ambitions. If you don't feel you deserve or are worthy of happiness and success, that's going to make it very hard to strive for them. As always, I'm not qualified to counsel you if you suffer deep-seated shame as a result of abuse or trauma – just know that everyone deserves help to overcome such feelings. However it is possible to be very hampered by feelings of shame if the family breaks up, for example, or you were involved in a significant failure at work, or you're drinking too much.

As with so many of these problem emotions, shame has a positive side. If no one felt shame, why would we bother to conform to cultural demands? The prospect of shame is one of the reasons we don't go round doing exactly as we please regardless of other people's needs. So the odd fleeting feeling of shame at behaving not very well is helpful in keeping us on track. The difficulties arise when the shame is strong enough to stop us socialising, or feeling confident about our ability to do our jobs, or relaxing around other people.

When we are children, the adults around us teach us to recognise a lot of emotions by naming them: 'I'm angry with you' or 'Are you feeling happy?' However shame doesn't get much of a mention. Occasionally 'you should be ashamed of yourself' but as a kid you often hear that when no, you're not remotely ashamed. As a result, we often fail to recognise shame in ourselves. But as always, recognising the problem is half the battle. So that's the first thing. If your sense of self-worth is lower than usual, and especially if you've recently had been part of a bad experience at work or at home, is this shame you're feeling? Recognise it, name it.

The issue here is that you've subconsciously taken one element of your life that you're not especially proud of and extrapolated it across your entire identity. Can you see that's an over-reaction? One technique that can work well here is to imagine it's not you but a close friend who is feeling like this. What would you say to them? I'll bet you wouldn't be nearly so harsh as you are with yourself, and it wouldn't change your view of them overall. So talk to yourself as you would to your friend, with a bit of compassion and understanding, and learn to be less hard on yourself.

> ## RECOGNISE IT, NAME IT

Think before you act

Impulsiveness is a recognised component of some neurodivergent conditions, although any of us can be affected. And some of us are impulsive in some situations while being considered and thoughtful in others. It can be a really useful trait at times – it's a big part of creativity for some people, and it's useful in a career where you have to take fast decisions, especially under pressure. When it's kept to a manageable level it can make you adventurous and exciting and spontaneous and unpredictable in a good way.*

But . . . maybe you spend impulsively and don't have the money for it. You're always in debt because you buy first and think later. Or perhaps you eat impulsively and your health is suffering. Maybe you make decisions before you really have enough information and it's got you into trouble at work, or you've done things you regret – sold the family car, got a puppy you don't really have the time to care for, started a business that is struggling to survive.

You can't change your underlying personality. Not only would you lose the benefits of being spontaneous, it just wouldn't be possible to stop being an impulsive person. What you *can* be is an impulsive person who learns to act impulsively less often.

Knowing yourself (Rule 37) is essential here. Once you identify the trait in yourself – whether it's in one particular area such as spending or across the board – you've put yourself in a position where you can tackle it. Next time you think about handing in your notice abruptly, or booking an expensive holiday, or getting a puppy, you'll know perfectly well you're on the brink of an impulsive decision you might regret.

I know that won't automatically stop you doing it – trust me, I know – but it does give you a much better chance. And the earlier in the process you catch yourself, the easier it will be.

---

* That's my justification anyway, being of an impulsive bent myself

Recognise what you're doing and you'll be far more likely to resist browsing holidays in the first place, which is much easier than stopping yourself when you're about to book the tickets. It's far easier to avoid going to meet a small puppy than it is to meet it and then decline to give it a home.*

And find strategies to avoid trouble in the first place. If you eat too much, or the wrong things, try not to have temptation in the house. That may mean being strict about never shopping for food when you're hungry. If you think these things through, you're much more likely to find a solution that works for you.

If you like to go shopping then set a budget, withdraw it in cash, and go out without any credit or debit cards. When the money runs out you'll have to stop. Or find someone boring and reliable to look after your credit card and refuse to hand it over. I don't say this will prevent every impulsive decision for the rest of your life, but this kind of strategy can make a big difference and turn a significant problem into the occasional hiccup.

> # THE EARLIER IN THE PROCESS
> # YOU CATCH YOURSELF, THE
> # EASIER IT WILL BE

* That's true for everyone, not just the impulsive among us

AT WORK

For most of us, our working life takes up a significant proportion of our time. And it's often a big part of how we define our sense of success. So feeling in control of our working life, and making sure it is going well, is essential to everything else.

Being in control means feeling that you can cope with the amount of work you need to get through. Of course there will be busy weeks, or days when you don't quite finish your to-do list, but you want to feel that you'll get back on top of it comfortably once the rush is over. However when you're really overloaded, you can find yourself struggling to cope. That can compound the issue and have an impact on the rest of your life too. So it's way better to keep on top of things in the first place.

Of course your wellbeing also relies on being able to manage work relationships. Not every colleague will be your best mate, and a few will wind you up the wrong way from time to time. That's all normal. However you need the skills to stop relationships becoming toxic or your boss persistently taking advantage of you, so that you can concentrate on your work and your career.

Another vital part of a successful work life is a sense of agency. You want to know where your role fits into the bigger picture, and to have some say in how you spend your time and achieve the goals you've agreed.

On the plus side, when everything is in harmony at work, it gives you a huge sense of wellbeing. And if things are tricky elsewhere in your life, work can become a sanctuary. So this section is all about how to stay on top of your work in order to feel successful all over.

Know why you're here

When you're up to your neck in alligators, it's easy to forget that the object of the exercise was to drain the swamp. As soon as work gets challenging or busy or pressured, the temptation is to firefight. There's a pile of stuff to do, and people shouting for action or decisions, and it would be easy to respond to the nearest request or the loudest demand.

But if you really want to be successful in your work, your career, there's a more important driver. In every job it stays pretty much the same, barring maybe promotion or a change of role, so once you know what it is you don't have to keep rethinking it. What is it? It's the reason you're here. The reason you're draining the swamp.

Why does your company employ you? Or if it's your own business, why is it here? It depends on your role, but here are some examples:

- If you work in sales, your job is to increase profits

- If you work in accounts, it's to ensure accurate and effective billing and payment systems

- In marketing, it's to increase customer loyalty and find new customers

- In production, to improve productivity safely

. . . and so on. That's your underlying reason to be here. The reason your job exists. It's why you come into work every morning. It's how the company justifies your salary. So work out what it is – even if you work in one of the departments I mentioned above you might feel your primary role is slightly different. That's fine.

If you're finding this tricky to identify, you could look at it this way. When you eventually move on from this job (hopefully upwards) what single thing would you hope to leave better than when you arrived? Sales figures? Safety? Productivity? There's your answer.

And boy, is this a useful thing to hold in your head at all times. In any job there are countless tasks that need doing, but lots of them make very little difference to your primary objective. Once you've identified what that objective is, it gives you a perfect touchstone against which to measure every task and decision, especially when you're under pressure.

That doesn't mean you never have to do any of the other tasks on your desk – completing forms, picking a venue for the training course, buying new office furniture – but don't waste time on them. If there's a sudden flurry of activity and some tasks will have to wait until things die down, these are the things that can wait. When it comes to delegating (more on that later) your primary objective will tell you which tasks are the most vital for the company. That will help you choose who to give them to, how closely to supervise and so on.

And at the end of the day or the week, when you're tired and wondering what you've achieved, this is how you can remind yourself that you're useful, you're valuable to the organisation, you're succeeding. Understanding your role and your importance – big or small – to the company is a vital part of job satisfaction, especially on those days when you feel you're struggling uphill.

> **IT GIVES YOU A PERFECT TOUCHSTONE AGAINST WHICH TO MEASURE EVERY TASK AND DECISION**

RULE 51

Stay pro-active

It's lucky we just established the real reason you're doing this job, because you're going to need it for this Rule. There are two ways you can tackle your job every morning when you turn up at work. You can keep things ticking over, or you can drive them forward. The people who really succeed at work are the ones in the second category. Of course there will be days when you're grateful that things aren't sliding backwards, but there should be more days when they're positively pushing forwards. Your figures are going up (or down I suppose, depending on your role), customer satisfaction is improving, innovation is high, productivity is up – whatever you're there to achieve.

The people who drive things forward at work are the ones who don't just sit there all day dealing with whatever arrives on their desk. However efficiently you do this, however good your working relationships, however well you keep on top of the load, in the end you'll never really succeed if this is all you do. You'll be fine, but you won't be the one whose name is always on senior management's lips, the one who is given the choicest roles, the one who is promoted every couple of years.

You have to make things happen. You have to create work – the right work. You need to come up with good ideas, and then put them into practice. You need to find ways to do your job better – reduce costs, increase profits, raise awareness, improve staff retention, attract new customers. These are the most interesting things to do, but they can easily get lost among the day-to-day reactive tasks that keep landing on your desk. So you need to make sure they actually happen.

It's self-perpetuating too because, once you get a reputation for creating real results, it will be much easier to keep doing it. Management will be keen to give you what you need – a bigger budget, another member of staff, a wider area to cover – once they realise you'll earn it back for them *and* some.

I hope you're convinced of the need to be pro-active, to think and plan and innovate, not just to react, or plough through the day-to-day stuff. Not easy finding the time though, is it? But that's what you have to do. You need to find a suitable time to do this, maybe ten percent of your time (more if you can manage it). That might be the first hour of each morning, or every Friday afternoon. Time you set aside to think, research, write proposals, plan for all those things that aren't going to end up on your desk unless you put them there.

Now you have to put that time in your diary, and stick to it. No good putting it in the diary and then ignoring it every time because your to-do list is still overlong, or some minor crisis has cropped up. The people whose careers thrive are the people who make this happen. Be one of them. Close the door, let the team know you can't be disturbed at these times. Or fix up planning meetings to drive the new ideas forwards. If you can, be out of the office at these times to keep interruptions at bay.

> ## THE PEOPLE WHOSE CAREERS THRIVE ARE THE PEOPLE WHO MAKE THIS HAPPEN

Be a free agent

One of the things that will give you a sense of satisfaction at work is the feeling you have some control. If you understand how your cog fits into the whole machine, whether you're a little cog or a huge one, you have a sense of purpose. You know your value to the organisation once you can see how it would suffer without you.

Of course this is easier in some jobs than in others. Generally speaking though, any boss should be pleased to be employing people who have an interest in the organisation and how they contribute to it, so you can always ask questions if you want to understand more about your role or your department's in the bigger picture. Equally, if your own team members want to know more about how they contribute to the company, give them answers. Like you, they'll be more productive and positive about their work if they can see where they belong.

The more control you have over your time and your work, the more satisfying you'll find it. The ideal scenario is one where you agree with the boss what needs to be achieved (your goals, if you like, in business speak) and then you're left alone to achieve it however you please. Obviously there will be parameters – time, cost, quality – and so long as you adhere to these you're a free agent. In many jobs you may even be allowed to work flexible hours or to work from home at least part of the time. All these things help to build job satisfaction and a sense of pride in your work.

If you work for yourself, you're already doing this. Then again, in some jobs, it might seem like a laughably distant dream. It's still worth recognising that this is the optimum way to get the best from you, or indeed anyone. A reasonable manager should at least listen, and they may be persuaded to let you do things your way at least in some small areas. Maybe they'll build from there.

If you think about how much agency you have in your current job, it should help you understand some of the reasons why you love it, hate it, find it rewarding, wonder why you bother. A sense of agency motivates pretty much everyone, but it matters more to some of us than others. If you're happy with the job you do, then don't let me put you off it. It's a precious gift to enjoy your work. If you don't enjoy it however, consider whether this is part of the reason. If so, and your boss isn't receptive, you might want to start considering whether you'd be happier elsewhere.

If and when you do move, this is one of the things you should consider about any new job you apply for. Find out about the company work ethos and how much say you'll have in how you manage your own workload. If you want not only to be successful at work but also to *feel* you're achieving, this is one of the most important ways to get there.

> THE MORE CONTROL YOU HAVE OVER YOUR TIME AND YOUR WORK, THE MORE SATISFYING YOU'LL FIND IT

Pass it on

If you are a manager, even at the most junior level, you need to make the most of the people on your team. If you can delegate successfully, you can create enough space to cope with your own workload and make sure you're not wasting time on things you don't need to. This will make you more productive and allow you to give the important tasks the time they need, all of which will feed into your ultimate success at work.

This might sound obvious to you, but what isn't always obvious is what delegating really is and how to do it well. Plenty of managers dish out tasks to their junior staff and think they're delegating. They're not. It's not delegating unless you also pass on responsibility for the task. In other words, remember Rule 52 and give your team member some say in how they get the thing done.

There's good reason for this. For a start, it will motivate them. And by giving them a measure of control, they won't keep pestering you with questions – they'll understand that if things don't go quite to plan they should use their own initiative (it's your job to let them know in what eventuality you would want them to consult you). All of this will help train up your team member so they'll be able to take on more demanding jobs for you, freeing you up for the vital work of the department, including that pro-active time you need.

So practise what we've just established in Rule 52. Agree with your team member what needs to be done, establish any constraints in terms of cost, deadlines and so on, and then leave them alone. Yep, get out of their hair. Of course you're still ultimately responsible for your department, and you want this job done well, so you'll make sure you delegate tasks that are within the capability of the person doing them, and that they fully understand what you're asking of them, and they have the budget, the authority and the time needed. Check in with them from time to time but don't interfere, or tell them how to do the job unless things are going very off course. Instead, sit down with them and let them reassure you things are under control, and tell you how they plan to deal with any glitches or modify their plans to accommodate any changes.

At the end of the task – whether it's taken a few days or has been a long-term project – sit down with them for a thorough review. Even if things haven't gone perfectly, find areas where you can give them recognition and praise. Discuss what they've learnt and what they might do differently next time. If things have gone seriously wrong, that'll be your fault. It will be because you delegated an impossible task, or you gave it to the wrong person, or you didn't give them the support they needed, or you weren't approachable enough, or you failed to monitor their progress. Or any combination of those.

Not a problem – just make sure none of those things is the case and it will be a great success. Good delegation is a real leadership skill and it will make your job way easier, and your team members will feel appreciated and motivated. So recognise it as a skill and learn to do it properly.

> # IT'S NOT DELEGATING UNLESS YOU ALSO PASS ON RESPONSIBILITY FOR THE TASK

RULE 54

Have a tidy desk

I hate this Rule. I so wish it wasn't true. I like to function in a state of organised chaos but sadly I have dragged myself, kicking and screaming, into the world of a tidy desk. I haven't extended this unfamiliar state of tidiness to much of my life, but in the interests of truth I have to concede that a tidy desk is a significant plus. There, I've said it.

So why have I given in to this state of affairs? I blame my wife. Every time I ask her for a piece of paper or some information she has written down, she reaches out and picks it up from her infuriatingly tidy and well-ordered desk. When she wants something from me, she'd ask and I'd waste two minutes here and five minutes there trying to find where I'd put it, finally unearthing it from under the rubble and helpfully passing it on to her. She'd thank me and then, irritatingly, follow it up by suggesting that if I kept my desk a bit tidier I might save us both time.

Eventually, after something fairly vital went missing for quite some time, causing a minor panic, I thought I'd shut her up by spending an hour making my desk tidier so she'd see that it didn't make any real difference. Unfortunately, however, it did make a difference. Not only did it save me time looking for things, I discovered that pausing to look for things on my desk interrupted my train of thought too. I didn't notice that until I stopped having to do it. To be honest I concentrate better as well, and I find that when I sit down at my desk at the start of the day I can get going much quicker when everything is orderly around me.

Research is quite interesting on this subject. A messy desk can actually help people who are really creative – and I still have a messy worktop out in my shed for example. However tidy desks are better for clear organised thinking. The exterior order of your desk helps your mind maintain internal order. That means your working environment is less stressful, which obviously means you can achieve more and feel more relaxed doing it.

The other advantage of a tidy desk if you work with colleagues is the message it sends out. If your work space looks an untidy mess, what does that say about your work? If it looks ordered and carefully thought through, it suggests you apply those approaches to your work as well. It's not only your colleagues and team members who will draw that conclusion, but your bosses too.

I do now keep my desk tidy because, after trying it, even I can see the advantage. I have two or three well-organised piles of paperwork at any time, a notepad and pen pot, a laptop, and somewhere to put my coffee down (that's obviously the most important thing). I also have a pin board for important long-term things like schedules, and keyboard shortcuts I never remember. The desk gets messier as the day goes on but I give it a quick tidy every evening before I knock off – because I do it every day it takes less than a minute. I just want to say though, the piles of paperwork might be organised but I don't stack them neatly. The papers are all askew and not lined up properly. Petty, but it's just as efficient and it keeps me happy.*

> ## THE EXTERIOR ORDER OF YOUR DESK HELPS YOUR MIND MAINTAIN INTERNAL ORDER

* And more importantly it winds my wife up

Control other people

One of the biggest reasons we don't achieve as much as we'd like is other people. They don't half get in the way. If it weren't for them, you'd get twice as much done, and you'd have been promoted ten times over by now. Unfortunately, however, almost all jobs entail working with other people – clients and customers, colleagues, bosses, suppliers. Obviously they can be useful sometimes, but you notice more the times they slow you down or hold you up or generally drive you mad.

It's hard to control other people completely, but with a bit of thought you can minimise the hassle they cause and still reap the positives. I can give you a couple of pointers but I don't know your job, so you need to identify where other people are getting in your way and come up with appropriate strategies to keep them diplomatically in line.

One of the near-universal difficulties of working with other people is interruptions. This is the main reason why working from home can be so much more productive in my experience. Partly it's the time taken up by people popping their head round the door or keeping you chatting by the coffee machine. But it's also what it does to your train of thought, and the frustration of being unable to focus properly on the task in hand.

Even if you work from home this can be tricky, and when I need to concentrate I usually turn off my emails and messages. Not only does this curtail the interruptions, it also means I can be confident I won't be disturbed.

Chatting at the office is an important part of working life for some people and is what makes the working day enjoyable. This might include you. So you have to find a balance between socialising and getting on with work. For a start, you can try to plan trips to the kitchen, reception, photocopier or whatever so they don't coincide with the most prolific chatters who are hard to get away from. Prevention is better than cure. Also do your best to socialise away from your desk so you can get away – it's much easier to say 'I must get on' and walk off than it is to get someone else to leave you. Have excuses ready if you feel you need them – 'I must get this email out before lunchtime' or 'the boss is shouting for the figures asap'.

If you have your own office, of course, you can shut the door, which is ideal. But don't overuse the strategy. If it's always closed, people will just knock or they'll never be able to speak to you. However if it's often open they'll understand that when it's closed they should wait. If they don't seem to get it, you can tell them politely but firmly.

One of my biggest gripes in every job I've ever done is people not getting back to you when they say they will. This can cause real problems sometimes, because it means you can't do your job properly. You can end up missing deadlines because someone else hasn't done their bit. I've already mentioned using your email 'sent items' folder to contain only emails that you need to chase up if people fail to respond. Not every communication is via email though, so you also need to note down in your diary when you need to chase people. If you chase them and they say thanks for the reminder and they'll get back to you, make a note to chase them again, and again, until they respond. If necessary, start emailing and copying their boss in.

If you have job-specific problems with other people hampering you and making it hard to do your job properly, have a good think about how you can minimise the problem. Ask other people for advice if you like – colleagues in the same boat or just friends you can brainstorm with. You'll be so much happier once you have a few reliable techniques that put you in control and let you get on with your job.

> # PREVENTION IS BETTER THAN CURE

Your diary is your bible

Even I have dragged myself into the twenty-first century and use an electronic diary that's synced across all my devices. And what a revelation! Hopefully you've done the same thing, because if you use it properly it makes it so much easier to manage your work life – and your home life too. That doesn't just mean it's less cumbersome, it means you can avoid most of those last-minute panics, missed appointments, diary clashes and all the other minor (hopefully minor) glitches that come with an old-fashioned paper diary. And remember, if you have a diary that is online and synced across your phone and your PC, or laptop, or tablet, you don't even have to worry about losing it.

Of course, it's no good just having the thing. You have to use it properly. Exactly how you manage the minor details of it can be quite personal, but you need to take advantage of its many useful features in order to get the benefit. If you aren't already doing this, it can take a little bit of practice but you need to persevere. The point about this kind of diary is it's not just a repository for information that you have to remember to look at. An electronic diary will actually do your remembering for you, as and when you ask it to. And reassuringly, you're in control of when it pings at you and when it doesn't. If you want a reminder, it will give it at a time of your choosing. If you don't, it won't.

For a start, you can view a day, a week, a month at a time. This makes it easy to see where you have gaps, and indeed how many gaps you have. So no excuses for not clearing the time you need for pro-active thinking and planning, for example. Once you've decided to block out every Friday afternoon, or the first hour of every morning, you can then mark that in the diary all at once for as far ahead as you like. Equally, you can see at a glance when you're going to be really busy and avoid arranging anything non-urgent during those few pressured days or weeks.

You can easily make sure that you set aside regular time for other things too. Dealing with emails, space for catching up with mundane tasks, preparation time for regular meetings. It's not just about the electronic medium, it's about making sure you schedule in all these blocks of time, whatever kind of diary you use. This is how you avoid all those panics and glitches and minor disasters that beset people without proper diaries. If you're asked to put together a paper or a presentation or to organise an event or run interviews, you can put in all the preparation time you need, at suitable points in the process, so everything runs smoothly when you get there.

If anything goes wrong, or you become overloaded at any point, or you don't have enough time to prepare for something, work out what's gone wrong with your system. Are you not reminding yourself of certain things far enough ahead? Have you allocated too little time for staying on top of the daily admin? Are you ignoring your diary when it tells you to prepare for things in advance? Work out what's gone wrong, and then do something about it. Or I can promise you it will just happen again.

We saw in Rule 55 that you need to chase people, and your diary will remind you to keep doing that – but only if you ask it to. From your colleagues' birthdays to booking annual maintenance visits, your diary can make your life so much easier in so many ways. The joy of a good diary is that you're in control of it, but with control comes responsibility. You have to take responsibility for feeding in the right information and instructions, in order for your diary to be the bible it should be.

IT'S NO GOOD JUST HAVING THE THING. YOU HAVE TO USE IT PROPERLY

Minimise meetings

One of the biggest barriers to getting on with your job can be meetings. And yet we keep organising them because they seem like such a good idea on paper. And to be fair, we've all attended meetings that were really productive and worthwhile, so we know it's possible. Nevertheless, you could do your job so much better and faster if you didn't have to spend so much time sitting around a table or in front of a zoom screen. You might not be in charge of many of the meetings you attend, but it's still worth knowing how to make them more effective and less of an impediment to working life. You may be able to instigate some changes now, and certainly as you move up in the organisation (you're a Rules Player, you'll go far) you'll increasingly be able to control the time you spend in meetings, and how worthwhile it is.

The first question to ask with any meeting is, is it even necessary? It's surprising how many meetings don't need to happen at all. The worst culprits, unsurprisingly, are the regular meetings. They happen simply because they always have. But every time, you should check through the agenda and see if this particular meeting needs to happen. What if it didn't? What if the agenda rolled over until next time? If you have, say, eight people in an hour long meeting, that's eight hours of other work not getting done, eight hours of pay being wasted.

Of course, a lot of regular meetings serve another purpose besides what's on the agenda. They bond the team, reinforce people's roles in the group. But what if your weekly meeting became fortnightly? And then there's meetings which are really only there to impart information. Could that not be done by some other means?

Even if this meeting is necessary, are all the agenda items essential? If you can shorten the meeting that will make everyone's jobs easier. So go through the agenda and see if there are items that are only there because they always have been, but aren't going to serve any useful purpose this time. Or are there items for information that could be sent round later? Or for discussion but actually you're not ready to make a decision yet because you're still waiting for some of the data to come back?

And finally, having cancelled any meetings you don't really need, and removed any agenda items that aren't going to be productive, the last question at this stage is whether all the people need to be there. Anyone who isn't going to contribute usefully, either during or as a result of the meeting, might as well be somewhere else getting some proper work done. If this is you, try to persuade the meeting chair of how much more you could do for the company if you weren't at the meeting.

Just because you, or someone else, needs to be involved, that doesn't always mean you have to attend the whole meeting. It's not practical to have people constantly turning up and leaving, from one item to the next. But there will be times, especially in long meetings, when the agenda can be organised so that certain people can leave part way through, or just turn up for one significant item. This can work particularly well with zoom meetings, where too many people easily becomes cumbersome and slows things down. It might even be better to hold a couple of smaller meetings.

By thinking through whether the meeting needs to happen, what it actually needs to include, and who really needs to be there, a huge amount of time can be saved for getting on with other things, instead of sitting round a table fretting about how much you could achieve if only you weren't here.

> # IT'S SURPRISING HOW MANY MEETINGS DON'T NEED TO HAPPEN AT ALL

Keep it quick

Great. You've cleared all the meetings you can out of the way, or persuaded the chair or your boss that you don't need to be there. But of course there will be other meetings you do need to hold. So here are some of the most useful tricks of the trade for making your meetings as brief as possible without being any less useful. That way, you get what you need from them, and you get back to your desk quicker to focus on the other important stuff.

First up, the agenda. This should have nothing on it that doesn't serve a useful purpose. No point aimlessly talking round a point and then doing nothing about it. The agenda should clearly state under each item:

- who will lead it

- how much time is allocated to it

- what the point of it is: information, action, decision (yep, those are the only options)

Incidentally, information should normally be circulated separately and only be on the agenda at all if it's deeply significant or confidential, or if people will need to ask questions. Don't send round information and then let people recap it for ages in the meeting. Or let people deliver information in a meeting because they haven't got round to circulating it. Make it clear that information must be circulated in advance and will only be added to the agenda in order to deal with questions, not to recap what everyone's already read.

Start your meetings on time. If people aren't there, they'll miss things. Don't go back over it when they arrive late – they'll have to wait for the minutes. No one will bother arriving on time if the meeting never gets going until ten minutes in, and how all that wasted time adds up. Once they learn you're happy to start without them, they'll start arriving on time. Trust me.

Introduce each item briefly, so people understand why it's on the agenda, and then remind them that they'll be making a decision, or deciding who will action the necessary tasks, or asking questions so everyone understands. Remind them too that you've given this item twenty minutes because it's really important, or this one three minutes because it's urgent but only a minor issue. That will make it easier to keep them on track and deter them from waffling on. If necessary you can interject and remind them you need to move on soon.

You need to set an example of being brief, not digressing into amusing anecdotes or going off topic, and this will make it easier to get everyone else to follow suit. The fact is, you're not the only one who has other things to be getting on with, and in the end everyone will be grateful for briefer, more effective meetings that last no longer than they have to. I've been part of groups that held smart, productive meetings where everyone was upbeat and could enjoy a laugh – just an on-topic laugh. A really good chair is like gold dust and if you can learn to run meetings that are brief and get the job done, you're already a success quite apart from what you can achieve with all the rest of your time.

> **START YOUR MEETINGS ON TIME. IF PEOPLE AREN'T THERE, THEY'LL MISS THINGS**

Avoid overload

I've already given you a whole section on how to make your time work for you. But look, streamlining your time at work is one of the very biggest factors in how successful you are. It doesn't matter how brilliant and talented you are if you never give yourself the chance to demonstrate it. You also have to be skilled at making the most of your day, your week, your month.

In any case, however brilliant you are, you still need a life outside work. Plenty of people manage to succeed at work, but only because they work late, and at weekends, and either take few holidays or work through them. That isn't healthy, it isn't good for your relationships, and it shouldn't be necessary. OK if you work in a theatre or a casino you'll have to work evenings, or if you're on oil rigs you'll be away for months at a time. But in the vast majority of jobs the aim should be to work smart and effectively, and pack up and go home in time for dinner. Weekends and holidays should be family and friends time, not keeping-on-top-of-the-job time.

So I'm going to pass on a few Rules about making the most of your time that are specific to your work, so you can achieve whatever you want in your career without being hampered by chasing your own tail half the time.

The first of these is a reminder that you really don't want to have the overload problems that necessitate using Rules 29 to 33 and thereabouts, which all help you get back on course. You don't want to go off course in the first place. You never want to be in a position of mild panic about how you're ever going to get through this pile of work, which seems to grow bigger faster than you can clear it.

You've already learnt a lot of the strategies for avoiding this scenario – keeping a useful diary and using it properly, setting aside time to be pro-active, clearing a space every day or week to keep on top of things, dealing with interruptions.

One of the biggest skills you're going to need is the ability to sidestep the things that you're not going to be able to manage efficiently. This can be tricky for the kind of optimist who always thinks everything will be fine. If this is you, listen extra carefully. You need to know what your limits are and don't take on work you can't comfortably manage – i.e. manage well enough to shine. That means don't volunteer, or do let the boss know that other elements of your work will suffer, or find something you can offload to make space.

This includes not generating work you can't cope with. When you proactively think up ways to do better for the organisation, not all of them will entail extra work, but many of them will. So when you put together your proposal, or plan the new strategy, you need to budget time as well as cost. If this can't be done without another member of staff, or without dropping an activity that eats up time, you need to be clear about that from the start and factor it in.

If you don't do this, you'll find your clever new ideas and strategies fall flat because they're never quite executed as well as they could be, and that will do nothing for your sense of achievement or your reputation. Better to do slightly fewer things brilliantly.

> # YOU NEED TO BUDGET TIME
> # AS WELL AS COST

Love the empty spaces

I've talked a bit about clearing space for this and that, but when it comes to work it's doubly important. In the normal way of things, the work keeps coming in. So if anything happens to reduce your capacity to deal with it, it will start piling up immediately. And something will happen to slow you down, even if you have no idea what it is.

Suppose your laptop crashes? What if your supplier lets you down and doesn't have the components you need in time? Maybe your colleague goes off sick at a crucial stage in your project, or there's a power cut and no one can get anything useful done for half a day, or one of your team hands in their notice unexpectedly. Maybe your car gets stolen and you have to take time out to talk to the police, or your dad has a health scare – you see, it doesn't even have to be work-related. And it might be just you that's affected, or it could be the whole team.

If you have no slack in the system, how are you going to claw your way back on top of the workload in the aftermath of this? With difficulty, is the answer. And sod's law, the next unforeseen minor crisis might happen tomorrow. You can't count on it to wait until you're back on your feet.

Assuming you've been listening up to now, and have started scheduling proactive time into your week, the danger is that this is what gives in an emergency. The trouble is that you can't afford to let this time get squeezed every time there's a minor crisis. Of course it might slip once or twice a year because you're ill, or it's the week of the big launch you've all been building up to for months, but otherwise it should be sacrosanct. If it isn't you'll find it gets worn away at over time until you're lucky if it happens once a month.

The answer is to make sure there's already a bit of slack in your diary. You should have a space for dealing with mundane tasks – it might be half an hour at the start or end of each day, or every Friday afternoon. This is the place to put in that extra slack. Suppose you arrive at work at 9 am, and it takes you about twenty minutes to get on top of everything and ready to start making calls, going into meetings, properly getting on with your day. In that case, don't schedule anything before 9.45 am. On a bad day, that gives you an extra 25 minutes to get back on top of things (and another 25 tomorrow, and the day after . . .). On a good day, you can just get cracking a bit quicker, or grab the chance to catch up with a colleague. If you've blocked in Friday afternoon for catching up and it's only Tuesday, you can take half a day now and give up some of your usual Friday afternoon.

If you're doing your job properly, it should never be a problem to fill a gap in the unlikely event you have one. You should always have pro-active projects in the pipeline that you can give some extra time to. And anyway, the phone will keep ringing and the email will keep pinging. So you really don't need to worry you've scheduled in more slack than you need.

> **SOMETHING WILL HAPPEN TO SLOW YOU DOWN, EVEN IF YOU HAVE NO IDEA WHAT IT IS**

Defer

I like the word defer. 'I'm deferring this task.' It sounds so much better than 'I'm putting it off'. It suggests you're being deliberate and considered, and so you should be. Knowing what and when to defer is a big part of doing your job well. I think we've established by now, if we didn't know already, that working life is punctuated by unexpected and time-consuming glitches and distractions and minor panics. You're going to build enough slack into your system to be able to weather most of these without too much trouble, but you'll still need to cope in the moment.

When trouble hits, there will always be some things that you do regardless – a big event or an important client meeting – and other things that you ditch. Maybe your lunch break or a final proof-read of your report. Everything that doesn't either carry on regardless, or get abandoned, is going to have to be deferred. That's just logic.

Maybe you'll be able to catch everything up tomorrow. But maybe tomorrow is a busy day, and perhaps the day after too . . . you're going to have to make decisions about what will need to be carried over beyond that. And that's where the deferring comes in. The deliberate and considered putting off, rather than just setting your to-do list on one side until you have time to deal with it.

When you hit these situations, you need to take five minutes to think about what you're deferring and how long for. You can address whole groups of things at once in a lot of cases – maybe you can catch up all your emails tonight or tomorrow morning, and that will do fine. Just check though – are there any that need a response this morning before you hold the rest over? Any that need a quick acknowledgement and 'I'm giving this some thought and will get back to you in the next few days'?

If you cancel your morning meeting, will that have any repercussions? If so will you cope with them, or could you make it a quick 15-minute meeting for the one agenda item that can't wait? And if so, when are you going to hold the rest of the meeting? Diarise it – this is why you have a bit of slack in your system. Just because it can wait until next week doesn't mean it can wait forever, so reschedule it for next week.

And consider the effects of your decisions on other people too. You might be happy to delay your team member's appraisal again, but how are they going to feel about it? And about you, if you keep treating them as if it isn't important? You might be happy to complete your report at the end of the month instead of next week, but one of your colleagues might be waiting on it before they can make a pressing decision.

So don't just put things off – defer them with care and thought. In a significant crisis of course you might not even be able to go through this process until tomorrow, but you must still do it as soon as you can. Otherwise things will slip through the cracks, and that will cause you even more problems down the line. You want to be one of those people who gets back in control effortlessly after a crisis, because you have provisions and systems and strategies for bouncing back almost immediately.

> # DON'T JUST PUT THINGS OFF – DEFER THEM WITH CARE AND THOUGHT

Spread the word

If you're in any kind of management position, one of the best things you can do is to teach your team these techniques for managing their time so they can achieve maximum success for minimum effort. Obviously this is a caring and supportive way to manage them, but it has plenty of benefits for you too.

For a start, as a manager you will be judged on the performance of your team. It doesn't matter how well you perform your own tasks, you're responsible for the results of the whole team or department. So you're not going to look good unless everyone does.

For another thing, your working life will be much easier if your team are relaxed and happy and feeling productive. You don't want stressed and irritable co-workers, you want to work alongside people who know, even in the midst of a crisis, that it's just a glitch and they'll be back to normal within a couple of hours or days, not frantically playing catch-up for the next week or so.

And on top of that, now you're working so much more effectively, just think what it would be like if everyone around you was doing the same? Always there with whatever you need as soon as you need it, before you have to chase, because their diaries are working properly for them. Never coming to you in a panic because they had to deal with that rush order yesterday and now they're behind with the week's figures. Suggesting to you ways in which the department could perform better, or pointing out how to cut down on the time spent in meetings.

So come on, instigate a whole new departmental style and teach them all how to stay on top of their workload. If anyone is struggling right now, you can schedule a half day or so for everyone to deal with all the little tasks cluttering up their desks and their headspace. Pick a day when no one has anything fixed in their diary, and keep it that way.

Now extend your half an hour or whatever at the start of the day for emails and phone calls to the whole department. No one schedules anything before, say, 10 am. The first hour of each day is for clearing the minor but necessary stuff out of the way (and not for idle chatting either). Not everyone is the same as you, so if this really doesn't work for some people you might need to be adaptable, but the principle is there, and the more everyone is in sync the better it will be. Of course there'll be the odd day someone has to meet a client at 9.15, or everyone is out of the office all morning, but once everyone discovers how productive the system is they'll want to make it work.

If everyone's desk is tidy, everyone will be able to work more effectively. However a desk is a very personal thing and, while it's a good aim to get every desk in the room tidy, you will need to recognise that some people are going to find this a struggle.* Be as encouraging as you can, but don't set people targets they can't achieve. It undermines their confidence in you and, by definition, it won't work. The point here is not to treat your team like children – it's to help them learn so you can all grow more successful together.

> # YOU'RE NOT GOING TO LOOK GOOD UNLESS EVERYONE DOES

---

* I'll be honest, I wouldn't have taken kindly to this in the past

Everyone can shine

One of the keys to success is your working relationships. The best environment for succeeding at work is one where everyone is positive and supportive, operating efficiently and giving each other the wherewithal to do their job. It's a virtuous circle. It's not smart to aim to be the only one who looks good. Not only is that kind of selfishness not Rules behaviour, it's also counter-productive. You'll look so much better if everyone is on side, helping you.

Clearly the very first step towards creating this kind of ethos is to be damn good at your job. Be honest – at least with yourself – about any weaknesses you might have and work hard to eliminate them. It's not going to help everyone else if you keep letting them down. Right, that's step one sorted.

We've already seen that if you have your own team, you want to teach them the strategies they need in order to be more effective. Having a collective time for catching up, helping them clear a backlog, encouraging everyone to keep their desks tidier. Don't preach, just let them see how their own performance improves.

The underlying principle is that if you help other people, they'll respond in kind. If you help people out at the last minute, or go the extra mile to get them the figures they need, or to set up a meeting for them, or let them use your office when you're out, you massively increase the likelihood that when the time comes, they'll return the favour. If you create a department full of people who owe you favours, you'll be perfectly placed next time you need an urgent favour from someone. You won't even be in their debt – it will just be evens until the next time you put yourself out for them.

You could say this is a cynical attitude. That I'm advocating manipulating your colleagues so they're obliged to help when you call in a favour, like some mafia boss. However I'm not suggesting you habitually say 'you owe me . . . '. in a threatening tone.

The aim is to foster a sense of community where everyone sees that by helping each other, everyone succeeds. It might start off as a two-way interaction between you and someone else, replicated across all your work relationships, but what you really want is for everyone else to be doing it when you're not even involved.

That's when you've really managed to create an environment where everyone is helping everyone else to succeed, if there's a crisis everyone mucks in to get it sorted even when it's not technically their job, and the job is much easier because all of that means things run more smoothly across the whole department. And on top of that, morale will be much stronger too.

Listen, if your whole department or section shines, don't fret that no one will see your part in it. Your bosses will credit you along with everyone else, and you'll also have plenty of opportunities to show them your individual flair – clinching a deal here, delivering a great presentation there, putting forward a proposal to speed up the system or save costs. So you can afford to be a rising tide that lifts all the boats.

IF YOU HELP OTHER PEOPLE, THEY'LL RESPOND IN KIND

We're all different

This Rule follows on from the last. As of Rule 63 you're going to help everyone else to succeed because you'll succeed along with them. You're going to give people what they need to do their jobs properly whenever you can, so everyone can perform at their best. And you're hoping they'll reciprocate so you can be more productive too.

Most of the time, this will work. It will work enough of the time to be worthwhile, certainly, although there might be the odd person who seems cantankerous and happy to accept support without apparently feeling the need to return it. This doesn't undermine the principle because these will be isolated people once the positive atmosphere is established. Nevertheless, the fewer grumpy sods the better, so it's worth cultivating these colleagues too if you can. The more people you can get on side, the better for you and everyone else.

The likelihood is that your grumpy sod is different from you in ways you may not have recognised. Our default is to treat others how we'd like to be treated ourselves, but some people don't want to be treated as you do. Give this person a bit of thought, and consider what it is that makes them feel comfortable, and whether you could accommodate them better.

I worked many years ago in a busy noisy sales office with an upbeat atmosphere. Everyone would share their big successes with the rest of the team when they came off the phone, and in a good week there'd be a running total of sales by Friday to see if we could beat our weekly record. All very jolly and positive and supportive and great for morale. Except for one person who seemed constantly slightly irritable and didn't join in, and whose sales figures were well below average too.

It turned out that this person was actually really sensitive to noise and hated being distracted by other people's mutual congratulations. Once this came to light, they moved to a desk in a quiet corner and became much happier. As was reflected in their improved sales figures. They continued to keep to themselves, but they relaxed and in their own way were as supportive as anyone.

Just because you, and the rest of the gang, are happy to work in a certain way, your grumpy sod might just be struggling to cope with the prevailing atmosphere. So think about it, and maybe talk to them. Or it might just be you, and not the overall environment. Are you giving this person what they need to do their job well? If you can make their life easier, they're more likely to make yours easier.

For example, maybe they like plenty of warning if you need them to find you data or figures or put together a proposal. You might be good at flinging things together at short notice, but research really isn't their thing and they need you to think ahead a bit and give them more time. Or perhaps they need more appreciation than you give them, or simply get really wound up when you use 'their' mug. So don't write off the workplace grump. Try to find out what's behind their unco-operative mood, and see if you can't change something to both your advantages.

> # THE MORE PEOPLE YOU CAN GET ON SIDE, THE BETTER

Be a good communicator

It's hard to achieve what you want to at work, and to do it in a happy and constructive atmosphere, without strong communication skills. The last couple of Rules have focused on how important it is to get everyone pulling together, all working on the same team in every sense. This is not only about how you give information, but also how you receive it.

In order to work well with other people, you need to be good at listening. That means be quiet long enough for them to put their point across – in meetings and in informal conversations – and actually take in what they're saying. It also means asking for feedback, about yourself or your ideas or your working style, and listening with interest to the response even if it's critical. Don't go on the defensive but genuinely think about what the other person is telling you. Even if you disagree, perhaps you can get a second opinion, or find a midway.

The other essential communication skill you need is to be able to brief people well. Suppose you're putting together an important paper for the board. You've asked one of your team to find you some important figures you need to include, which you have to drop in before you deliver the thing at the end of the week. The figures land on your desk on Wednesday and, aaargh! That's not what you asked for! You needed the figures for last year broken down by month *and* by product line . . .

Hang on. Why would your team member have given you the wrong figures? Presumably they will have believed they were giving you the right ones. But what they heard isn't what you said. That's your fault, that is. It was your job not only to let them know what you needed, but also to make sure they understood. If you didn't do the second bit, that's your bad. And now your report won't be on time, or won't be accurate.

You might be despatching your team member to cover for someone in another department, asking them to gather information for you, tasking them with running an event, getting them to purchase equipment. Whatever it is, you need to brief them properly or you could end up having to sort out a mess that you don't have time for and is ultimately your responsibility. So here are a few pointers. Clearly the time you spend on this will vary, but the principles are the same whether you're putting them in charge of a big event or project, or simply asking them to do some quick fact-checking for you. If the results matter to you, do it properly.

- The first thing is to brief your team member at a time and place where you can both concentrate, whether that needs two minutes or half a day.

- Now tell them what you need them to do, as clearly as possible, and give them some context. If you'd told your team member *why* you needed the data broken down by product line as well as by month, it's much more likely they'd have understood that it needed to be done.

- Ask them to feed it back to you to be sure you're both on the same page, and speaking of being on the same page, write it down or email a summary for anything more than a quick task.

- Next, give them the parameters. The budget, the deadline, the degree of accuracy required. And let them know what level of decisions you're happy for them to take themselves, and at what point you'd want them to refer back to you.

- Finally, check whether they have any questions for you, and let them know you're happy for them to come back to you if questions occur to them later.

If you've done all that – properly – it won't be your fault if it goes wrong. But if you've done all that properly, why would it go wrong?

> ## IF THE RESULTS MATTER TO YOU, DO IT PROPERLY

RULE 66

Be unremittingly cheerful

Yes, I know this is easier said than done. And you might be wondering how being cheerful even in adversity is going to benefit you. The answer is, you succeed or fail largely on the basis of your working relationships. Not only the mutual support I've been highlighting, but also the way you're seen by your bosses, senior management, anyone with the power to promote you. Or not promote you.

You know as well as I do that the bosses have a pretty good idea how everyone behaves when they're not there, so it's not good enough to put on a happy face when they're in the room. Word gets back. Besides, you don't want to be two-faced – charming in front of the boss and short-tempered when their back is turned. You want to be consistent and respected by everyone, regardless of who is in the room.

Now you might be a born optimist, or you might struggle with worry or low moods, for example – something we've already looked at in Rules 39 and 47. And this is why you want to do your best to conquer them. Because even if it doesn't come easy, your career is going to benefit hugely if you can learn to be positive and upbeat when you're at work. (Actually, if you can make it a real habit, you'll reap benefits beyond just your career.)

If you can be the person everyone can rely on to lift morale at work, to cope in a crisis, always to be looking for solutions instead of giving up, you'll earn huge respect. People will know where they are with you, and it's a place they're happy to be. Everyone values consistency and optimism. Not overbearing jolliness – you don't want to trample on other people's concerns and tell them not to be silly. *They're* allowed to be worried or upset or overwhelmed or negative. But you're a Rules Player, so you're not. You will be reliably positive, always confident there will be a solution, and life's too short to let things get to you. You don't have to be extrovert and bumptious. Best not, in fact. You can be quietly positive if that suits your style better.

So now, people will come to you knowing you won't be negative or snarky or defeatist or short-tempered. If they've made a mistake, the sooner they tell you the better, and the way to ensure they do is to get a reputation for helping to get things sorted, rather than tearing them off a strip. Equally, you want a reputation for not passing on gossip, so that your team members and colleagues feel they can confide in you if they're struggling and want your support.

Look at the role you've carved out for yourself. You'll be respected and admired, people will come to you in times of crisis or trouble because they know they can count on you to boost their mood and help gets things sorted. Everyone is your ally, so they'll help you when you need a favour. The boss can see the dynamic and recognises your talents with people, and your contribution to staff morale.

> # YOU SUCCEED OR FAIL LARGELY ON THE BASIS OF YOUR WORKING RELATIONSHIPS

DECISIONS

It's generally not hard to decide whether you're in the mood for a cup of tea or not. Some decisions are pretty straightforward and you don't need my help to make them. However, if you're deciding whether to move house, or accept a promotion, or choose a school for your kids, or ask your elderly parent to move in with you, things can get a bit trickier.

This kind of decision is going to make a big difference to your life, perhaps for a long time. You want to get it right. And what's more, you want to feel confident that you're getting it right. Not only will the right decision enhance your sense of success in life, the wrong call could really set you back, financially, emotionally, professionally and physically. At least that's the worry – and it's that anxiety about whether you're doing the right thing that really gets in your way. The stress of making the decision can end up being more detrimental than the actual outcome, whichever option you choose.

What you need is a set of Rules that will do two things for you. Firstly, they'll guide you through the process of making decisions so you arrive at the best solution. And secondly, they'll give you confidence that you're choosing right, so you're not hampered by worry or indecision. And the encouraging thing is that the process of making a confident decision is pretty much the same regardless of what the decision is about.

Any decision is better than none

Here's the first thing you need to understand when you put off or delay making a decision, not because you're waiting for necessary information but simply because you're not sure what decision to make. I'm here to tell you – that's a decision in itself, a decision to defer or delay, and it's wasting you time without achieving anything useful.

Whether you're deciding when to tackle something, or wondering how to deal with it, or indeed when things first arrive on your to-do list, you need to understand that indecision is the enemy of efficiency. A lot of time gets wasted in putting off decisions that seem difficult and, while some of them are important enough to think hard about, many of them simply waste your time.

Think about the life cycle of some of the paperwork that arrives on your desk or doormat (or the emails in your inbox). You open it and read it. You're not sure what to do with it so you leave it alone or put it in a pile of papers. Next time you go through things, you read it again, are still unsure, and put it back on the pile or leave it in your inbox. Maybe even move it to another pile in a speculative kind of way. This keeps going until eventually you decide it's not important, or it's too late now anyway, and you put it in the bin. Or file it. How much of your time has that one email or letter taken up? How many times did you read it – or at least skim it? And why? Simply because you didn't make the decision straight away to file it or bin it.

Here's another scenario. You need to book a venue for a work event. However you can't do that until you have made certain other decisions – maybe how many people will be invited, or what sort of catering you'll provide, or where the best location is. If you dither about these choices, by the time you're ready to book the venue your preferred place is no longer available. Or wherever you book has loads of questions about food and seating arrangements and budget and so on – all of which are now urgent because you left it so late, so the whole thing is stressful and you're under pressure. And it's your own fault.

You need to be able to make decisions as fast as possible. Sometimes that's still quite a while, because they're important and there's lots of information to gather. But once you have that info, just get on with it. And think about how much it really matters – for all those minor things getting the decision made can matter a lot more than what the decision actually is. After all, you're not an idiot, if the choice is obvious you'll have made it, so how much can it matter?

Do I want tea or coffee? Should we mail round our customer list on Monday or Tuesday? What colour shall I paint the bathroom? Where shall we go on holiday? Which of these designs do I prefer? Every time you dither, you create more work and reduce the time you have to do it in.

Look, not making a decision *is* a decision. It's a decision to defer things. You're not avoiding a decision when you procrastinate – you're just making a different decision, as well as the one you're eventually going to have to make anyway.

> ## NOT MAKING A DECISION *IS*
> ## A DECISION

Pick apart procrastination

You might be a serial procrastinator, or maybe you rarely put off decisions. Either way, procrastination can be a huge barrier which, at its worst, stops you getting on with your life. It can hold you back from changing jobs, moving house, having kids, committing to a relationship. Even smaller decisions can really get in your way, quite apart from all the time-wasting we saw in Rule 67. So why aren't you getting on with this decision? What's worrying you?

You need to answer these questions in order to be able to unblock the process. Hey, I can give you some Rules in the next few pages that will really help you make this decision, but first you need to understand your own hesitation in order to overcome it. So let's take a quick look at some of the usual suspects.

- You don't know where to start. This can be a problem with big or complicated decisions – for example you're thinking of moving location, so do you pick the location and then find a job, or vice versa? If you really can't work out where to start, just start anywhere. Research areas to move to, or look at what jobs seem tempting, just do something and you've made a start.

- You don't have enough information. That's easy – you need to work out what's missing, and go and find it. Just be sure this isn't really an excuse for some other psychological resistance to making a decision.

- You need to resolve something else first. Maybe you've decided you definitely want to relocate, but you need a job first. Good – go and find the job then.

- You're daunted by the whole prospect. You want to make a decision because you're not happy with how things are, but you're finding the whole thing overwhelming. But as we've seen, you're making a *decision* to do nothing, and it's a decision you know is the wrong one, so anything has to be better. In this situation, focus on just taking the first step, and then the next, and so on. Avoid looking at the whole big picture until you can cope with it, but this way you're still making progress.

- You're not certain how you feel. Which job to take, which area to relocate to, whether to end this relationship? Think about how you feel in the current scenario, and then visualise yourself in the alternative situations and really try to get a sense of how they feel.

- You have an underlying problem you're not addressing. This isn't so unusual – for example, you can't quite get your head around you and your partner living together because deep down you're not sure you actually want to be with them.

Maybe your blockage is different again. Once you recognise that something is holding you back, it shouldn't be too difficult to identify it. I'm no psychologist, but if you routinely procrastinate over decisions – or even just one big decision – and can't get to grips with it, you might find some professional help useful to get to the bottom of it.

> ## YOU NEED TO UNDERSTAND YOUR OWN HESITATION IN ORDER TO OVERCOME IT

You're on your own

I've touched on this before, but you need to get your head around the fact that no one else can do your decision-making for you. Of course you can delegate the less major work decisions to someone else, along with the responsibility for the area in question. And of course a group of you can come to a collective decision. But most decisions have some kind of emotional component, and that's the bit that only you can do.

You could argue that all decisions have an emotional angle or they're not decisions, they're simply logical conclusions. And strangely researchers have found that in rare cases where someone has no emotional responses – which can occasionally happen following brain damage, for example – they are unable to make decisions. Or, of course, to care whether they make the right one, which can be part of their problem.

So all decisions require some level of emotion, and if the decision is yours, the emotion needs to be yours too. We often consult other people – friends, colleagues, experts – before we commit to a decision. That's fine, and often very helpful, but you need to be aware of what input you're asking for and what its limits are. The danger lies in setting too much store by other people's advice.

Suppose you're trying to decide where to go on holiday, to take a simple example. Everyone you consult will have an opinion. They might suggest a particular location because they had a great time there, or some other spot because there's loads to do, or another destination because the weather is reliably warm. You can see how they're all being influenced by their own emotional responses – one loves hot weather, another likes having plenty to do, and so on. They're also influenced by their own experiences. They'll recommend places they've enjoyed visiting, and not ones where they had a less good time – even if the reason for that was something that won't apply to you. Maybe they were going through a bad patch with their partner, or the hotel they stayed in was rubbish, but it will likely colour their advice.

It might be less obvious how the people you talk to are being swayed by their own emotions and past experiences, especially if it's a decision that seems on the face of it to be very practical, for example at work. However, even when you can't see it, emotions and past experiences are playing a part.

Consulting other people can be helpful of course, but you have to understand this flaw in the system. It means that there's always the possibility that what's right for you isn't going to be what seems right to other people. Don't make the mistake of doing what they say simply because they say it. It might look like the easy answer, but that doesn't make it the right one.

So be brave enough to make a decision that's out of kilter with other people's advice, so long as you recognise why that is. Maybe you know that you're the type to regret a thing you haven't at least tried, or that you wouldn't be put off by a bit of discomfort, or that for you the long game is more important. Understanding this should give you confidence in your own gut feeling, even when it goes against the advice. It should also make you wary of setting too much store by other people's opinions even – especially – when the decision is a really big one.

> IT MIGHT LOOK LIKE THE EASY ANSWER, BUT THAT DOESN'T MAKE IT THE RIGHT ONE

You're not alone

Ha! I'm messing with your head now. I just said you're on your own, and now I'm saying you're not. Well look, it was an important Rule that, unless a decision is expressly shared by a couple or a committee or a partnership, you're on your own. It's your decision and you can't duck that. However, now you understand that you aren't sharing the final decision with anyone else, we can talk about how other people can contribute.

Just because the buck stops with you, that doesn't mean you can't consult. It's a really useful part of the process in lots of ways. For a start, some decisions can feel quite lonely. Well, maybe that's because they are, but it can still be comforting to feel you're not on your own. For example, single parents can find it really daunting to make choices for their kids like which school to attend, or when they're old enough to stay out with their mates overnight. Rule 69 told us that you can't just ask your mum to decide for you, but if you talk it through with her, at least you'll feel a bit less alone. That has a value, especially when you understand why you're doing it, and follow Rule 69 so you won't be overly swayed by her.

Maybe it's not you that needs to feel supported. Maybe it's them. If someone else is going to be affected by your decision, consulting them is a really good way to get them on board. Even if you don't make the call they want, at least they know they've been listened to (you're going to listen properly, aren't you?). And they may raise points you hadn't considered. Your colleague might draw your attention to the fact that any decision you make about speeding up delivery times will have knock-on effects for accounts. Your teenager might point out that if you move to the other end of town, they won't be able to get to football training during the week.

Other people are really helpful for prompting you to consider options or outcomes you hadn't previously thought about, and for asking you the questions you hadn't thought to ask yourself. You might talk to a specific person precisely because they have past experience. You can ask them not only what happened but why they made that choice, what they'd advise you to consider, what they'd do differently another time. Just remember that they're not you, and the situation will never be identical. To give you a crude example, we all know investments can go up as well as down. Take two people, one who's money grew and one who lost money, and ask their advice about investing, and you'll likely get two different answers. They can't both be right.[*]

So input from others is helpful, but it's just another tool in the box. It should inform your choices, but not determine them. It can be a good idea to consult people you know will give you differing views – you might have to work quite hard to unpick the lessons from it, but it makes it much easier to be your own person when you commit to a choice.

A word of warning here: there's a danger of putting off a decision by telling yourself you haven't consulted everyone yet. But actually there comes a point when no one is really adding anything you haven't heard before, and that's the point to stop – you should by then have talked to the key people who will be affected.

> # SOME DECISIONS CAN FEEL
> # QUITE LONELY

---

[*] Although they could both be wrong . . .

Know what your decision is for

I know, you're thinking that you must be aware what the decision is if you know it needs to be made. But not so fast. Too many people get this wrong and end up making a choice that doesn't serve them well. Why? Because they focus on the means rather than the end. Let me give you an example. Let's suppose you're applying to university and trying to decide on a course to do. You might think that the decision here is to pick a course, but first you have to get your head round why you even want to go to uni.

Are you trying to get the best degree you can, at the best uni you can, so you have your pick of the jobs when you graduate? Or maybe you're already confident what career you want and need a course that is tailored to that specific path. Then again, you might be less worried about what happens after you graduate, and more focused on finding a course in a subject that really fascinates you. Or maybe you don't really know what you want, but three years at uni should be great fun and a degree of any kind at the end of it seems like a productive way to spend that time. Maybe it's really about the location and gives you a reason to try living away from home, or in the big city.

You see? How can you possibly decide on the right course until you've got your head round why you're going to uni? Obviously more than one of these reasons might apply, but probably not all of them. The best way to arrive at an answer is to keep asking yourself 'why' until you arrive at the real end point. 'Why do I want to go to uni? In order to study. Why do I want to study?' And so on.

I'll give you another example. You want to move your small business to new premises. Why? It might be so it's nearer home for convenience, or because you need somewhere bigger, or because the rent is too high, or because you want to be closer to a key supplier. Keep asking why until you arrive at the answer. Suppose you want to be nearer home? In that case, maybe you could leave the business where it is and move home. Or not, but you need to go through the 'why' process in order to consider this possibility. Or why do you need somewhere bigger? Depending on the answer you might realise there are other options – a second premises nearby, or outsourcing certain functions.

If you don't go through this process, the danger is that you enrol on a uni course that doesn't really do it for you, or move your business into new premises that don't help with your commute or your supplier issues. Of course often there's more than one motivation behind a decision, and that makes this process doubly important. You don't want to focus everything on solving one issue and overlook another or you'll find yourself in new premises that are more affordable but leave you no room to expand, or studying a course you love but being unable to get a job that inspires you afterwards.

> KEEP ASKING YOURSELF 'WHY'
> UNTIL YOU ARRIVE AT THE
> REAL END POINT

Set parameters

Right – we're making progress. You can't make a good decision without knowing what constitutes good. So now you know why you're making this decision, it's much easier to gauge if you're making the right one. After all, decision-making would be easy if all you ever had to do was find a solution – any solution – and Bob's your uncle. But it's more complicated than that, because there may be lots of answers to your dilemma but not all of them will do. You'll have boxes you need to tick, so this next stage is about identifying those boxes.

For almost any decision, project, plan, event there are three key boxes or constraints:

- cost

- time

- quality

If you have several options on the table, it's likely that you can rule some out because they cost too much, take too long, or don't give you a good enough result. Occasionally one of these factors won't matter, but they're a good starting point. You can say that in order for your decision to be a good one it must cost less than this, or deliver by then, or meet that quality standard.*

However, you might have any number of other parameters, so this is the moment to clarify what they are. If you're choosing a uni course, you might want it to be within three hours' travel from home. If you're moving your small business, you might need to find somewhere that can connect to the fastest possible internet.

---

* If a publisher comes to me for a book, I like to tell them they can have two out of the three, and they can pick which two. It amuses me to watch them trying to choose

If you're picking a supplier for a key component, it might have to be someone who's happy to work on 60 days' payment.

The sky really is the limit here. It's not about inventing parameters for the sake of it – far from it, because the more there are, the trickier it can be to find a solution. However, any genuine constraint can and should make it on to the table. If you're buying a car and can't countenance one that doesn't make your dog wag its tail excitedly the first time she sets eyes on it, then that's a valid constraint. I might think you're making it harder for yourself, but if it's that important to you, then it should be one of your tick boxes.

One important point: these are firm parameters, not preferences. You might also have a separate list of preferences, and that's fine, but don't make things harder by telling yourself your new house must have four bedrooms when you could manage on three. The box it has to tick here is three bedrooms. If there's a choice of suitable three-bedroom houses, one with an extra bedroom might clinch it, but if you end up with a three-bed house it will still be a good decision. Likewise a supplier who is nearby might be preferable but, so long as they still tick the boxes for cost, timescale and quality, it's not essential.

By the time you get to this stage you should be feeling much happier about your decision even though you haven't made it yet, because you can see exactly where you're heading. Getting to this point can take a few minutes or several months, depending on the complexity and the importance of the decision, but the steps are the same either way.

THERE MAY BE LOTS OF
ANSWERS TO YOUR DILEMMA
BUT NOT ALL OF THEM WILL DO

Manage the facts

You're not going to make a decent decision if you don't have all the relevant information. Sometimes this is a really quick process, and fairly instinctive, but you're still assembling facts. If you're shopping and meal-planning, you consider options and rule them in or out almost without thinking, but only because you already have the facts you need – the cost, how long it will take to prepare, the fact that one of your teenagers said they'd be out tonight and another won't eat chicken. You see? Your day is full of minor decisions you don't even notice because you have all the facts. Along with others where you have nearly all the facts, but just need to message your partner to check what time they'll be home, or look in the fridge to see if there are any tomatoes left.

But what if you're making a big decision at work about a new project, or you're trying to decide whether to build an extension, or retrain for a new career? This is where not focusing on the process can really hold you back. I know a couple who procrastinated for literally years about revamping their kitchen. They knew they really wanted to do it, but they had no idea whether it was feasible to move their range cooker and flue it out of a different wall. All they needed was to recognise this was information they needed and to get someone round who had the expertise to answer the question. But instead they hit a kind of inertia and didn't even start on the project they'd spent years saving up for.

Not having all the facts is one of the biggest causes of procrastination. The solution is to identify what facts you need, and then go and get them. It sounds straightforward but most of us subconsciously shelve decisions from time to time because we haven't recognised that this is why we aren't taking them. The other risk of course is that you go ahead and take the decision but without assembling the information you need first, and then it turns out to be the wrong decision. If that means you have to have a salad without tomatoes in it, it's not the end of the world.

But what if it means you sign a big deal with a customer and then discover they're planning to pay you 90 days after delivery, and you haven't got the cash flow to cope?

As with your parameters, there will be information you must know before you decide (such as the payment terms) and information you'd prefer to know (like the tomatoes). Information you'd prefer to know will help you make up your mind, but it won't be a deal-breaker. Either of these categories might include other people's views — not for advice, but because the decision will affect them in some way and it's important to know that it will keep them on side.

The other reason to split the information you need into these two categories is it's easy to become overwhelmed by too much information. You're surrounded by uni prospectuses, kitchen brochures, supplier catalogues . . . you can feel so paralysed by it all that you struggle to decide. In that case, focus on identifying the 'need to know' facts so you can clear your head and stay in control of the process. Don't use the mountain of information you have as your starting point, use the list of facts you actually need.

> # NOT HAVING ALL THE FACTS IS ONE OF THE BIGGEST CAUSES OF PROCRASTINATION

Count your chickens

Let's recap – you're doing really well so far. Here's what you've achieved:

- You've identified the decision you're actually making

- You've used that information to set all the parameters you need – and some non-essential preferences

- That's enabled you to work out what information you need

Excellent. You know what you're doing and you have all the necessary information to make this decision. You know what? You're nearly there.

In fact, for smaller decisions, once you reach this point you might feel able to make a decision on gut instinct. That is to say, gut instinct informed by all this thinking and information-gathering you've done. Occasionally there will now clearly be only one option left, which makes things simple. But for the majority of the most important decisions, you need to be more thorough about the process. So what you need to do now is to identify the remaining options – all the possibilities that tick the essential boxes, and hopefully satisfy a good few of your preferences too.

You might think you can see the options in front of you that meet all your requirements. But the really great decision-makers don't stop there. This is one of the things that separates the truly successful from the rest of us and enables them to make decisions we wouldn't have thought of. Because this is where you get creative.

Before you move on to the stage of picking the best choice, let's see if you can't find some other options to consider. Put on your thinking cap and generate some new and innovative possibilities. Even if you do have tomatoes in the fridge, you could experiment with your recipe anyway. If you've created a job description for the new post, are there other options if you took on part-timers or flexiworkers? How about using two different suppliers, one for the smaller components and another for the main parts? What if you take a gap year before you go to uni, and get a job in hospitality to see if it's really what you want to do?

This is the time for coming up with exciting solutions because now you know what you're doing, and why, and what all the constraints are, and you have all the facts at your fingertips. So this final stage before you actually make the decision is the moment to give yourself the widest possible range of options that all fit the bill. That might be two or it might be ten – it doesn't matter, because at this point they'll all be good.

And never forget, as we saw earlier, that doing nothing is a decision in itself. That means it's usually one of the options on the table too, unless there's a big reason why it really isn't an option. For example your landlord is selling up so you *have* to find a new flat, or your current supplier has gone bust. Sometimes it might even be the best option – when it's an active decision and not an unconscious default – so remember to keep it on the list if it meets your criteria.

> # THE REALLY GREAT
> # DECISION-MAKERS DON'T
> # STOP THERE

Weigh it up

This is where you do the pros and cons thing, although a simple list of pros and cons isn't always the best approach so there are other helpful processes you can try too. Sometimes the answer is clear, or the decision's not important enough to agonise over for hours. But when it really matters to get it right, it's worth thinking it through in a few ways.

Pros and cons is definitely one of those. A list of arguments for and against can help you see things in a fresh light. However, a lot of pros can outweigh a single con, or vice versa. Do you fancy jumping out of a plane without a parachute? On the plus side it would be exciting, invigorating, the view would be great, it would take your mind off any other worries . . . and there's only one con I can see. But it's a pretty big one.

One of the most useful ways to evaluate your various options is by considering the risks and rewards. So for each possibility, make a note of the best and the worst thing that could result from it – not from the overall decision but from this specific option. Maybe there's a risk production will grind to a halt, or there's a potential to go way over budget, or you'll drop out of uni. Then look at the plus side too – costs could come right down, productivity could double, you could come out with a top degree. But wait a minute, that's not the whole story. Maybe there's a tiny risk that the production line will stop, and a high likelihood that costs will plummet. Or the other way round. So you have to balance the risks and rewards together with the likelihood of them happening.

If these two processes haven't pointed you towards a single decision, they should at least have narrowed the options. Let's see if we can reduce them further. The risk/reward thing is useful but not very nuanced, so now think through the consequences – good, bad and in between – of each option. Stick to known consequences, not possibilities. For example you know this will squeeze your budget this much, or that will be logistically simpler, or someone will hate this particular option. You'll need to do this for all the relevant areas: consequences for the budget, the timeline, you, the department, the family, the production team, and so on.

Here's another way of looking at things. Ask yourself what you'll regret most if you take each option, and what you'll regret if you don't take it. This can be particularly helpful when you're measuring several options against each other – job candidates, suppliers, career options, extension designs.

Of course you're not going to go through all this palaver just to decide whether to have a cup of tea. But understanding how each method works, and being familiar with them, means that even when a decision doesn't warrant weeks of heart searching, you'll have developed a sense of which technique is helpful for what kind of decision. Sometimes you'll sit down with pen and paper and draw up risk and reward lists, or pros and cons. Other times it will become almost instinctive and you can run the options through these filters in your head.

By the time you've gone through all of these thought exercises, you should have a pretty clear idea of which decision is the right one. And if, after all this, you still have no front-runner, then how much can it really matter? After the last few Rules you're in a place where all options fulfil the objective and tick all the boxes, and none has any red flags attached or this Rule would have spotted them.

> ## ASK YOURSELF WHAT YOU'LL REGRET MOST IF YOU TAKE EACH OPTION, AND WHAT YOU'LL REGRET IF YOU DON'T TAKE IT

RULE 76

Consider your feelings

One of the challenges with decision-making is working out where your feelings fit into the equation. We've already established that you can't make good decisions without any emotional input. And of course, some decisions are all about your feelings. From whether to move in with your partner to what colour to paint the bathroom, feelings are almost the only factor. You might want to check it works financially, or consider how much natural light there is, but the whole thing is basically a 'what do I want?' decision.

However, maybe you don't know what you want, and that's your problem. You're torn between being around the person you love and being independent. Or you're fed up with your job, but do you really want a career change? In this case, a useful technique is to ask yourself questions and observe your feelings as you answer them. The 'what will I regret most' if I do or if I don't is a good place to start. You can also ask yourself questions along the lines of:

- what's the worst that could happen if . . . ?
- could I change my mind later if I do/if I don't?
- what if I hit money problems?

Sometimes a good friend can help with this, especially if you let them know you want them to ask questions that help you explore scenarios you might not have thought of.

It also helps to consider if there's an underlying worry that's putting you off. One of the ways to identify this is to ask yourself, 'why haven't I already moved in with them/handed in my notice?' This might highlight why you're hesitating so you can deal with it. You can also think about the current situation – because doing nothing is a choice – and what is holding you where you are now. Job security? You like your independence? If you know this, maybe you can find a way to change things for the better without having to forgo the benefits of the current situation.

At the other end of the scale are the decisions that aren't about your feelings. Workplace decisions, for example, shouldn't generally be about you, but it can be hard to be dispassionate if you have a vested interest. Perhaps you're in charge of the departmental relocation plans, and you really don't want your office anywhere near a particular colleague who drives you barmy. Or you've been asked to propose a way to reduce company expenses, but you really don't want to have to start using cheap hotels for business trips, or to give up your company car. Or the most promising option was proposed by someone from a rival department.

It can be genuinely difficult to make decisions that disadvantage you personally, while benefiting the organisation. If you can find a way to keep your office at a distance from your irritating colleague that honestly makes no difference to the company, I can't really see the problem (although don't dump them on some other poor sod who's going to struggle). But where there's a conflict, you have to pick the option that works for your employer. That's what you're paid for. So imagine the cringe-making moment when your boss questions you about why you haven't suggested using budget hotels, with a knowing glint in their eye. Then visualise them congratulating you on a top decision, recognising that it can't have been an easy choice for you personally. Find the motivation to do the right thing. And, of course, remind yourself you're a Rules Player.

ASK YOURSELF QUESTIONS AND OBSERVE YOUR FEELINGS AS YOU ANSWER THEM

Have a Plan B

Some decisions get made and then they happen. You decide to appoint a new sales person, and you appoint them. But other decisions are speculative – you decide to bid for this contract, or apply for that course, but obviously in these situations you might not get what you decided to aim for.

Maybe you just move on to the next contract or apply for a different course. Maybe you applied for several and you'll just pick the best one you get offered. However sometimes you've really set your heart on a particular course or career or job application, or thrown everything at clinching this particular deal.

Clearly on a practical level, if it doesn't happen, it doesn't happen. But on an emotional level it can be quite devastating. It's not only the effect of being told 'no', it's also the stress you go through waiting for the answer. Perhaps it's the months of hanging on for your A-level results, desperate for the grades you need to get on to that course. Even if you do finally get what you need, you've still had months of agonising waiting. And if you don't there's a whole new decision waiting for you as you work out what you're going to do instead.

Back when my kids were of an age to go from primary school up to secondary, the parents spent months debating which schools to apply for. You can't often be sure your child will get in because the good schools fill up and there may not be enough places, so everyone is on tenterhooks for months and weeks leading up to allocation day, when they finally get to find out if their child has got into their chosen school.

One of the things I noticed was that there was a clear divide between how the parents coped with this. One group would fret and worry and panic, and the others would be a bit anxious but basically pretty sanguine. What will be, will be. So what was the difference between these two sets of parents? Well the second group all had a Plan B that they were basically happy with. Obviously they preferred Plan A (by definition) but they knew they could live with Plan B. They had been to look at plenty of schools, they'd visualised their child in all of them, they'd considered the upsides, and they'd put down second-choice schools – maybe thirds too if necessary – which were perfectly liveable-with. The panicky parents had staked everything on their favourite school and hadn't thought through what would happen if their child didn't get in. Some had not even put down alternatives because they couldn't countenance it. But that really doesn't help you if you don't get the school you wanted.

So the moral is always have a back-up to get you through the wait, as well as to give you an alternative if your plans don't work out. The more important your Plan A is to you, the more you need a Plan B. That way you can sleep at night while you're waiting to find out what fate has in store.

> # THE MORE IMPORTANT YOUR PLAN A IS TO YOU, THE MORE YOU NEED A PLAN B

Simplify the complex

One of the most complicated decision tangles I remember was a friend of mine whose son was coming up to the age to move schools. She was thinking about moving back to London (where she'd lived before) and also thinking about cutting down her working hours so she could retrain. Of course, she'd need to decide what to train in, and the options were different in London from where she was living at the time – as were the school options for her child.

Aargh! Where to start with all that? She had several decisions that all depended on each other: a school for her son, where to live, whether to retrain, and if so in what – which was contingent on where she was living. While this was a particularly tangled set of choices, it's not that unusual to find yourself having to make an intertwined set of decisions. One of the biggest problems can be that you just don't get round to making them at all because you can't figure out where to start or how to go about it.

Maybe you've been offered promotion, but you have an idea for setting up your own business, which would mean handing in your notice at work. In order to make the business viable you'd need to create a workshop space at home so you could run it from there, but you're also thinking maybe your elderly mum should come and live with you, although you'd have to create more space for her, which might put paid to the workshop plans. This kind of complex group of decisions can be really overwhelming because all the individual decisions feed in and out of each other.

OK, don't panic. They way to deal with this is to put any decisions you can into sequence. Take a deep breath and think about this . . . You need to decide whether to start your business *before* you can decide whether to accept the promotion. After all, the promotion is irrelevant if you're going to leave anyway. So focus on the first decision – whether to start your own business.

Now you've simplified matters and you're left with two main decisions – whether to set up in business, and whether to ask your mother to move in. Until you've got those two sorted out there's no point considering if and how to reconfigure the house, so that can wait for later.

Now try to make each of these two decisions as if the other one wasn't there. If you decide *either* that moving your mum in isn't the best decision *or* that you're not ready to start your own business, the house rejig stops being a problem. It's only if you decide yes to both that the house thing needs addressing. If that happens – well, then you've made a decision about your mother, the new business and the promotion (by default). So you only have one decision to make, which is how to organise the living arrangements to fit your mum and your business into the house.

That's much simpler, and you can get creative about maximising the space in your house, or about you moving in to your mum's, or both of you moving to somewhere new. That's nothing compared to the tangled knot you started with. The key is to work out the sequence before you start worrying about the decisions themselves. Generally you'll realise one thing is more important and eclipses everything else, or there's a logical order which unpicks the knot.

PUT ANY DECISIONS YOU CAN INTO SEQUENCE

Commit

Once you've refined all the options down to one that is clearly better than the others, your decision is made. Lovely when that happens, isn't it? Of course quite often it isn't quite that simple. Maybe there are still a couple of possibilities left, or maybe none of them looks great. But a decision has to be made – even if that decision is to leave things as they are – and you need to get on and make it. There's value in simply having a decision at all, so everyone knows where they are and can get on with their life and their work.

Actually, any choices still standing at this point are adequate at worst. And maybe you're in the enviable position of having to choose between two excellent options. If there's really nothing to choose between them, then flip a coin. You might as well – it's a dead heat. And sometimes, for an emotionally charged decision, tossing a coin has an extra benefit. If you catch yourself hoping it comes down heads – or tails – there's your answer regardless of how it actually lands.

Whether you care how the coin lands or not, and whether this is a choice between fantastic options or a least worst option, you have now made your decision. All you have to do now is to implement it.

And now here is where people too often go wrong. Once you have made the decision, based on all the facts, all the rational arguments, all the relevant opinions and feelings – your own included – you have to stick to it. If you don't, you undermine the whole process, and your own authority, as well as rendering the whole exercise a massive waste of time, whether that was an hour or several months. And perhaps more importantly than all of that, you undermine your own confidence. You've been through a thorough process, you've considered everything you needed to, and now you need to believe in yourself and your decision.

Remember why you're reading this book? You want to be in control of your life, to focus on the areas you want to achieve in, to glide smoothly and effortlessly through work, home, family life, to be successful. That's not going to happen if you keep raking over past decisions, questioning yourself, tweaking things you need to stand firm on.

Maybe it's not your innate self-confidence, maybe it's other people telling you they think you did the wrong thing or questioning why you made this decision. Look, you need to let them see that you absolutely know you've made the right choice. You can explain it – not defensively, mind you, but to help them understand. This can be tricky if you made the decision on a whim, but if you've been following these Rules you will have very good reasons for making the call you did. Even if it's a least worst option, you can demonstrate why you ruled out all the other choices.

So don't make those important decisions without being certain they're right. And then having made them, commit one hundred percent, and don't look back.

> # NOW YOU NEED TO BELIEVE IN YOURSELF AND YOUR DECISION

Work together

Where a decision is primarily a practical one – picking a supplier, for example – the process we've just explored should get you to the right answer. Failing that, it will narrow it down to a couple of options either of which is pretty much as good as the other. But what if you're not alone – what if you're working as a team, and you can't agree? In fact, looking at the options the right way will often show you which is best.

I remember being on an interview panel where we had narrowed the candidates down to two, who were both impressive and very different from each other. One of my colleagues said 'It's impossible to see how one is better' than the other', to which I replied 'Oh, one is definitely better'. 'Which one?' she asked, to which I had to say, 'I've no idea at the moment, but one is definitely better'. I suggested we go back to our original job specification, because while both candidates had significant strengths, one of them was bound to match what we were actually looking for better than the other. If we couldn't choose it was our fault for losing sight of our objective. Sure enough, one met the criteria we had set out more closely, so that's the one we appointed.

Even when you're making a decision alone, this is obviously an essential thing to do when faced with two options: remind yourself what you were actually trying to achieve. If you're working in a partnership or a team it not only helps you ensure you make the right call, it's also a very good way to reach agreement. You set your criteria collectively, so you should be able to pick an option objectively that meets them most closely.

Joint decisions can be tricky, whether you're on an interview panel or committee, or running a business in partnership. That's what makes it extra important to go back to your original aim – if you can find an objective best solution, you'll be able to agree on it. But what if you can't?

I've owned a business with someone else, and our solution was to have clear lines of responsibility – this can work for parents sometimes too. My partner and I discussed all the big decisions together, but we both knew that in the rare event of a stalemate, it was my call if it related to sales or finance, and my partner's when it came to marketing or production. While we occasionally disagreed, it never became acrimonious and this was a big part of that.

If there is an uneven number of people, a vote will decide it, although it's always better to reach a strong majority – ideally a unanimous decision – without the need for a vote. The really important thing, though, is that whatever your individual view, you commit to the group decision. Sometimes you have to grit your teeth, but you're a Rules Player so you can do that. Inside the group you might politely express your reservations, although you'll never say 'I told you so' if things don't work out.* Outside the group you never let your wider colleagues, customers, suppliers know that the decision was anything but unanimous. Just as, in family decisions, you and your partner might disagree privately, but you always present a united front to the children.**

> # YOU SET YOUR CRITERIA COLLECTIVELY, SO YOU SHOULD BE ABLE TO PICK AN OPTION OBJECTIVELY

---

* *The Rules to Break* Rule 74
** *The Rules of Parenting* Rule 39

Find common ground

Rule 80 works well for practical decisions, but what about emotional ones? These tend to be personal and usually, if there's joint responsibility for the decision, it's between you and your partner. Maybe you really can't agree about some aspect of raising your kids, or perhaps one of you is miserable where you're living now but the other really doesn't want to move.

In many ways, of course, this can be a relationship problem. However if you make sure you always put each other first* it should happen only occasionally, and over things you both feel equally strongly about. It would be strange if it never happened at all though, even in the strongest relationships.

If you're putting each other's feelings first – which is a brilliant and essential relationship Rule but you *both* have to be doing it – that will resolve almost all of these issues. You'll end up with those great couples conversations that go, 'If that's what you'd like, that's what we'll do'. 'No because you don't want to, so it's fine . . . '. Where there's a practical element to the decision, if you really can't both see the same answer, how much can it matter? If you love your partner, why not let them have what they want?

But we're all human, and sometimes you'll embarrass yourself by getting a bit petty about what kind of car to get, or how to decorate the hallway. One option here, as with the more practical decisions, is to have your own areas of authority. In many traditional couples, dad made the important financial decisions, and mum had the final say over how the kids were raised. This can work well, even if this particular division of responsibility is a bit old-fashioned for your family.

For anything that you haven't divvied up in this way – and indeed anything you have which your partner nevertheless feels strongly

---

* *The Rules of Love* Rule 26

about – you should focus on compromise. Always look for a middle way that works OK for you both, even if it's not perfect for either. If one of you has your heart set on a particular kind of holiday, at least let the other pick the accommodation or the dates – or both. If you can't agree on how to decorate the hallway, give yourselves each the right to veto up to three colours or styles (or one, or four – I don't care, it's your hallway).

The important thing here is to care more about your partner's happiness than about what colour the hallway is. In a strong relationship you won't emotionally blackmail each other or try to get your own way by bursting into tears. You'll want to find a solution. And if you *want* to reach a decision you can both buy into, you will. Where this rarely happens, and you often row about relatively minor decisions, my advice is to attend to the relationship before you start worrying about what colour to paint the hall.

> # IF YOU *WANT* TO REACH A DECISION YOU CAN BOTH BUY INTO, YOU WILL

HEALTH

You know how much easier it is to get through your day when you wake feeling fresh and raring to go. So it's no surprise that it's trickier to get through your life successfully if you spend much of your time not quite as healthy as you could be. Just a bit below par.

Of course there are illnesses and injuries that are beyond your control, but a great deal of how you feel is down to your behaviour and your choices. The way you eat, sleep, drink, move and generally function on a daily basis can make a huge difference. I know, finding the time in a busy life to change things isn't easy. And you may be reading this nervously thinking I'm going to tell you to spend an hour a day running or in the gym. Well don't panic. For one thing, I'm not going to tell you to do anything. It's your life and you're in control, so you don't have to do anything anyone else says, and that includes me. That's the point. Besides, recommending you make changes that are unrealistic is just a waste of paper.

All you need really is an increased awareness of which differences are worthwhile, and some nudges that help you focus on the things that will have an impact. This is about the everyday improvements you can make to your overall health that will give you back a sense of being in control, and mean that most days you wake up ready to face the world and tackle whatever your day throws at you. It's these – often small – changes to routine that help give successful people the extra ten percent that sets them apart.

So take a look at the next few Rules, and see if you can't raise your health baseline so you're better equipped to cope with every aspect of your busy life.

Think your body healthy

If you're not a big fan of being overtly sporty, and you don't want to take up running or football or going to the gym on a regular basis, you've come to the right place. I'm with you. Like you, I want to be healthy, and I'm always keen to find small changes that will make a noticeable difference, but I don't want to rearrange my diary permanently to make space for things I don't particularly enjoy. So changes I can make in my head are right up my street.

None of us wakes up every single day feeling physically one hundred percent. Bits of us might hurt (if you're still young, trust me, this gets worse), or we might be coming down with a bug, or we have a bit of a headache. At this point, you have a choice. You can let it get you down and interfere with your whole day, or you can carry on regardless.

As I say, the aches and pains become more frequent as you age, and as your body takes longer to heal from any knocks and injuries. So if you allow them to spoil your day, life is going to get worse as you get older. But even when you're young, if you spend your day feeling like rubbish because you've got a bit of a cold, or you've turned your ankle, that's a day when you're not going to be your best, at work or at home. If the illness lasts a few days, you'll have been off your game for a week. That's not the easy, successful passage through life we're looking for. And to be honest, if you've already got a stuffed nose or a headache or a dodgy ankle, you don't deserve to be feeling down as well.

So don't. Learn to brush these things aside and don't let them affect your mood. You can have a great day at work even with a headache, or a fantastic weekend with the family despite not being able to put much weight on your ankle. It's all in your mind, and it works a lot like affirmations. If you tell yourself – and anyone else who asks – that you're fine, you'll feel way better than if you tell yourself that you're having a bad day. It's self-fulfilling.

Separate your mind and your body. Just because your body is feeling below par, it doesn't mean your mood has to follow suit.

It's a family joke that if ever my mother-in-law has a bug and you ask how her cold is, she'll reply 'What cold?' I have another friend who, when I asked if her arthritic back hurt a great deal, replied 'Oh it doesn't hurt. It just aches, that's all.' The fact is that both of these people remain cheerful despite their various gripes and pains, which is where we all want to be.

Of course this is much harder with significant disabilities, and clearly there will be days when you can't manage it. You shouldn't have to make the effort, but it will help if you can find a way. I used to have a friend who had had both hands amputated and was always cheerful (I can't speak for how he felt when he was alone). If I tried to sympathise with him, he told me off firmly and pointed out that plenty of people were worse off than him. I appreciate some of us are born more cheerful than others, and of course this will be harder if you suffer with low moods and depression. But I'm just here to pass on what I've observed, and all I can tell you from experience is that if you can manage to follow this Rule, you'll find life much easier.

I would also add that this isn't about being in denial and pretending your body isn't below par. That isn't necessary, and you need to acknowledge the physical problem in order to ease it or medicate it or whatever. It's simply about refusing to allow it to influence your mood, and downplaying it – without denying it – is the best place to start. Tell yourself it doesn't hurt, it just aches. Or you're not coming down with flu, you've just got a bit of a bug. Something and nothing.

SEPARATE YOUR MIND AND YOUR BODY

Think your mind healthy

It stands to reason that if you can master Rule 82, and feel physically better just by convincing yourself that your aches and pains aren't so bad, you should be able to do the same thing for your moods. And indeed you can. Rule 47 – if you can remember back that far – was about coping with low moods. But of course if you can avoid them in the first place, or at least minimise them, that has to be even better.

Again, I'm not qualified to prescribe strategies for clinical depression and other conditions that require professional intervention, so this is about those occasional doldrums we all run into. They might last half a morning, or they might drag on for a couple of weeks. And they bring with them a feeling of flatness, where it's hard to find the energy to do much that isn't just routine.

Wouldn't it be great if they never happened – or at least happened less often, and for less time? In many ways, half the battle is recognising when you hit these phases. Maybe there's an underlying stress or worry, which may help you notice the effect on your mood, but it might just be hormones or the phase of the moon or something equally hard to identify. So learn to recognise the symptoms. Our problem of course, in terms of success, is that you lose some of your zest for life, which means everything takes more effort, and you're less inclined to be pro-active and to drive forwards with the things that matter to you.

Can you use this as a clue? Do you find yourself inclined to cancel social engagements or skip out-of-work activities, or are you struggling to be pro-active at work, or finding excuses not to phone your mother? The level of doldrums we're talking about here should be sortable, but only if you recognise it, so practise spotting the indicators that make you think, 'Aha! Doldrums!' Then you can get on and do something about it.

Rule 47 gave you some practical strategies to approach this, especially if there's an external cause you can address. However if you can catch it early, simply shifting the way you think can make a big difference. Now you know what's going on, tell yourself it's just one of those low ebbs and it will soon blow over if you take no notice. The way to counter a drop in mood is to do something that reliably lifts you, so tell yourself, 'It won't last – I'll knock it on the head by listening to my favourite pick-me-up music'. Or going for a walk on the beach (if you're lucky enough to have that option), or fixing up to see a particular friend this evening, or watching your favourite comedy on TV, or doing some exercise.* Whatever you know lifts you. If you tell yourself this will work – and believe it – it almost certainly will.

Sometimes the solution is to indulge it, but do it positively. So take time out – a day, not a week – but frame it in a positive way. Don't tell yourself you'll spend the evening doing nothing because you haven't the mental energy for anything else. Instead tell yourself you'll deal with it by taking an evening out to be self-indulgent and curl up on the sofa with a favourite movie, so you can recharge and be raring to go tomorrow.

> # PRACTISE SPOTTING THE INDICATORS THAT MAKE YOU THINK, 'AHA! DOLDRUMS!'

---

* Not my preferred solution thanks, but it might do it for you

Eat yourself healthy

If your diet isn't as good as it could be, are you aware of just how much difference that can make to your life? There's a huge body of research now that links your diet to how you feel, and if your energy is low and your health is poor, your path through life will be harder. There are plenty of websites and books that will give you loads of information about what foods are healthy and what aren't. I'm just going to give you a few pointers that might help.

I think you know perfectly well whether your diet is healthy. If you're already eating an excellent diet, you can skip this Rule. If you need to keep reading, be reassured there are ways of adjusting your diet that don't involve giving up everything you love and replacing it all with chia seeds and kefir. Nor do you have to become vegan or follow any kind of fad diet. All of these are options, but none of them is compulsory.

As a broad principle, I'm against fad diets. I'm against dieting generally in fact. The reason for this is that I've seen countless people do it – I've done it myself in the past – and although there can be excellent short-term benefits, they don't last. It's not helpful to eat healthily for a few weeks. You need to eat healthily for the rest of your life. So you need to make changes that are sustainable. Permanently. That might mean going slowly. If you change just a couple of things and then, once they become habit after a few weeks, you change another couple – and so on – it might take a bit longer to reach a healthy diet, but once you get there it will be a habit, and one you can maintain for good.

So what are you going to change? You need to look at what you eat now and decide what are the worst culprits (clue: processed foods) and what you're not eating enough of, which might be fresh vegetables, or it might be proteins, or maybe oily fish. It's probably the vegetables, let's be honest, but there might be other things on the list. Go online or buy a book if you want more information about which foods are good and bad.

Now resolve to tweak this over time. Cut out this and add in that. After a couple of weeks cut out something else and add another good thing. But look, this is less about what you put in your trolley and more about your eating habits. It's no good buying loads of healthy veg and then picking up a pizza on the way home from work every night, while the veg all rots in the fridge.

Why do you do that? I mean, why do you buy so many takeaways? That's the habit you need to pick apart. If you're always too exhausted to cook when you get home, think about foods you can have waiting that take no effort. Or is it that you're so hungry as soon as you finish work, because you tend to skip lunch? So take something to work that you can eat at your desk, which will keep you going until you get home. Maybe start by aiming to cut down the number of takeaways, before trying to eliminate them. In any case, never tell yourself you've given anything up for ever. That's an impossible target to achieve and when you fail you'll ask yourself 'what's the point?' and stop trying. Just cut down, as far as you can cope with.

So analyse your less healthy habits, and look for solutions to the underlying reasons for them. Why don't you eat enough veg? If you don't like them, or you can't be bothered to prepare them, find solutions. Ready-prepared veg aren't as good for you as fresh veg, but they're a lot better than fast food. You're looking for improvements, not perfection. Once you start to reduce the less healthy elements of your diet, you can add in some more healthy ones, whether that's chia seeds and kefir, or an apple and a handful of nuts.

> ## YOU'RE LOOKING FOR IMPROVEMENTS, NOT PERFECTION

Everything in moderation

This Rule applies to what you eat, as we've just seen. The aim isn't to excise everything unhealthy and never eat it again. You want a basically healthy diet but if someone offers you a chocolate, or once every two or three weeks you buy a takeaway or eat at a fast food chain, it's fine. If you're otherwise eating healthily. The problems only come if the chocolates and fast food start to become too frequent, and begin to affect your energy levels, your health, your bank balance . . . your life, in other words.

There's no point in a long healthy life if you're not enjoying yourself. There are lots of fun things you can do as much of as you like – hanging out with your friends, going for walks, watching movies, reading books, tinkering under the car bonnet, painting – and others that have their limits. That doesn't mean you can't ever do them, but be aware of the negative effects.

Alcohol is a good example. The occasional drink, when you're not driving, is fine for most people. A couple of drinks maybe. Perhaps just occasionally three or four if it's a big occasion. But too much alcohol makes you feel rubbish the next day. Even a lower level, if it's almost daily, is bad for your health and makes you less productive, not to mention less fun to be around in many cases.

Coffee is another case in point. One of my family is a bit of a coffee snob and likes to have a really good coffee every day.* However he restricts himself to two cups a day maximum, and never in the evenings, because he recognises that if he has more than that his mood suffers, along with his sleep and possibly the quality of his work.

---

* I say 'really good' because he says it – personally I can't tell the difference

It's not only what you consume of course. It's how you spend your time. Too many late nights – regardless of how much alcohol is involved – can get in the way of the rest of your life. Look, if you're serious about being successful these things are important. Your career will always go better if you restrict the late nights to Fridays and Saturdays, than if you stay out late midweek. Your relationship will go better if you don't indulge in some kind of hobby that means you hardly see your partner. Video gaming for three hours a night, for example.

It's not easy to be honest with yourself about when you're doing too much of a good thing. But as with so much of being a true Rules Player, self-awareness is at the heart of this. Only you can really know where the tipping point is for these things, from something you can enjoy healthily to something that undermines other parts of your life, your work, your relationships. And if you're serious about achieving the most out of life, you need to draw yourself a line and not cross it. Occasionally – as with tobacco and alcohol for some people – that means giving it up entirely. Mostly it means doing the things you enjoy, but in moderation. That's not so bad, is it?

> # AS WITH SO MUCH OF BEING A TRUE RULES PLAYER, SELF-AWARENESS IS AT THE HEART OF THIS

Move

I've been saying that I don't enjoy exercise but that's not actually true. What I dislike is organised exercise. I get that some people really enjoy it, and that's great, but I'm not one of them. I don't want to go to classes or visit the gym three times a week. It's just not for me. If you can't imagine a life without this kind of exercise, you probably have this Rule covered already and can skip to the next page. However, if you're like me, you and I need to find ways to get a healthy level of movement into our lives without having to go for a daily run or join the local volleyball team.

I think we all know that moving more is better for us. It keeps us flexible, helps keep our weight healthy, and keeps the whole body functioning better. It means we can cope better on busy days, or when we have to run for a bus, and will help us to stay healthy so we can enjoy the rest of our lives with ease.

So, if we don't want to do the organised exercise thing, we need to find alternatives that achieve the same effect. We need to move about, sometimes in ways that get our hearts pumping, by doing things that we enjoy enough to stick with them. There's no point deciding to go for a daily run if you're going to give up after a week. If you can stick with it, brilliant, but if you can't, it's a waste of time. Not only that, you'll feel bad about not keeping it going, and that won't help you.

The people I know who stay active without doing organised exercise have all found things they enjoy that just happen to require exercise. That's not why they do them, it's just a convenient by-product. I know lots of people who enjoy walking – they wouldn't do it for its own sake, on a treadmill, but give them an attractive location and they'll go for a regular walk. Some only enjoy it in company and find someone to walk with. Some get a dog, who I guess fills that role nicely.

I also have friends who enjoy gardening. Not just a spot of light deadheading, but gardens or allotments that need some pretty physical work to keep in order. Digging, staking, pruning and so on. Several people I know do their own building – renovating the attic, building an extension, knocking two rooms together, refitting their kitchen themselves.

And then there are the little nudges that all build up. When I worked in London on a daily basis, and commuted on the Tube, I always walked up the escalator instead of standing still while it carried me up to street level. I used to work in a second-floor office and took the stairs, not the lift. Little things, but I did them every day. Not to mention options like seeing how many press-ups you can do waiting for the kettle to boil, or always taking the stairs two at a time, or playing frisbee with the kids. The smaller the nudges, the more of them you'll need to keep healthy (obviously). On the other hand, the easier they might be to build into your routine so they become just habit.

So if you don't want to Exercise with a capital E, that's fine. Just make sure you have plenty of other ways to keep yourself moving so you stay fit and active and able to enjoy life.

> **IF WE DON'T WANT TO DO THE ORGANISED EXERCISE THING, WE NEED TO FIND ALTERNATIVES THAT ACHIEVE THE SAME EFFECT**

Be able to sleep

We've never going to manage seven or eight hours' sleep *every* night. There's always the occasional night you get disturbed, or can't drift off, or have to be up early. That's normal. But far too many people struggle with long-term reduced sleep. Chronic insomnia needs medical support to deal with, and there are also lots of useful websites, books, articles and so on to help you get back into a healthy sleep pattern.

My job here is to make sure you understand why it matters. It's not enough to think it's normal given your job, or your stage in life, and you can cope. Coping is not good enough if you want the energy, the mental alertness, the positive mood, the good judgement, to be successful. If you're serious about taking control of your life and smoothing your route to happiness and wellbeing, you have to prioritise sleep.

The disadvantages that come with being tired don't go away when you think you've trained your system to cope with never quite getting enough sleep. You might have reached a point where you often aren't aware that you feel tired, but the symptoms will still be there:

- poor attention
- impaired reasoning and judgement
- low mood and/or depression
- anxiety and stress
- poor reaction times
- weakened immune system
- health problems such as fatigue, poor co-ordination and weight gain
- lower libido

That's not a comprehensive list, that's just a few examples. How is your life going to run smoothly when you have all that – and more – to contend with? It's not, is it? So if you're routinely missing out on sleep, remedying that has to be top of your agenda. You can't just catch up at weekends, as the experts will tell you. That's not how it works.

The very first thing to do is to make sure that your regular routine gives you time to get enough sleep, and that includes time to prepare for it – a hot bath, or some relaxing music, or whatever helps you to drift off. If you can't get up later in the morning, you'll need to go to bed earlier, even if that means curtailing week-night evening activities so you're home in time. You're aiming for at least seven hours sleep each night, so maybe eight hours between when you get into bed and when you get out of it again. Then give yourself an hour before that to wind down and prepare your body and mind to sleep – you know how everyone says not to get small children excited just before bedtime? Well that goes for the rest of us too. So don't eat and drink, exercise vigorously, watch horror movies.

If you have nowhere near this amount of time for sleeping right now, try bringing your bedtime forward by about 20 minutes every few days until you hit this target. Once you're doing this properly, I hope things will improve all round. And at least if you do still have other sleep problems – difficulty drifting off, or staying asleep – you'll have vastly reduced the potential causes and made it a lot easier to address the problems.

> MAKE SURE THAT YOUR
> REGULAR ROUTINE GIVES YOU
> TIME TO GET ENOUGH SLEEP

RULE 88

Catch some sun

Here's a great way to stay healthy, which few people would argue with. Our planet's energy comes from the sun, so it seems unsurprising that our own energy levels are directly influenced by sunlight, as well as through all those indirect means such as the food we eat. Spending time in the sunshine has a positive effect on your health in all sorts of ways and is one of the pleasantest ways to stay healthy.

For a start, almost all of us find our mood lifts when the sun comes out. That's not a coincidence, because sunlight increases the amount of serotonin we produce – a hormone which helps us to feel calm and happy. So seek out sunshine when you can – take your morning cuppa outside on a sunny day, or pick your time for a walk when the forecast is for sun, before the clouds come over. Maybe you can choose to work outside, or get off the bus or train a stop earlier if it's sunny so you can catch some rays as you walk. Even rolling up your sleeves makes a difference because it increases your exposure to the sun.

Of course you want to avoid being out in the sun for too long if there's a risk of burning, so depending on where in the world you live, and how susceptible you are, you'll need to take this into account. However the advice is that little and often in the sun is better than staying out for hours at a time in any case. Here in the UK, you're unlikely to be able to spend too long in the sun during the winter, so the more of it you can grab for the cooler six months of the year, the better.

One of the biggest health benefits of sunshine is that it's the body's best way to get vitamin D, which we produce ourselves in reaction with sunlight. In the UK very few of us make enough vitamin D through the winter, although our bodies store much of what we make in the summer. You can take a supplement of course, but it's far better to be making your own if you can – it's not in enough foods for most of us to be able to get what we need through diet alone.

And how is vitamin D going to make you more successful? Well, it's good for your bones and your muscles, and for your immune system. Anything that helps your system protect itself against colds and bugs has got to be a good thing, surely, and higher vitamin D levels correlate with fewer colds according to the scientists. It also reduces symptoms of depression, and there's an increasing amount of research indicating that vitamin D also plays a part in reducing dementia. And all of this for free! Just by going outside and soaking up the sunshine. Apparently morning light is particularly good, and just ten minutes walking to the bus stop or sitting outside with a cuppa can make a real difference. There aren't many things this good for your health that require you to do a thing that costs nothing and makes you feel great, so you'd be mad not to find ways to build it into your life as often as possible.

EVEN ROLLING UP YOUR SLEEVES MAKES A DIFFERENCE

Laugh at yourself

Now here's a Rule for being healthy that I find easy to follow, and no shortage of material for either. I talk to myself a lot – I'm sure we all do – and I'm always ready to poke fun at myself or have a laugh at my own expense. Only today I couldn't quite see into my coffee mug to check if I'd finished drinking it so I tipped it towards me. The answer was no, I hadn't finished it. As a result I poured it all down myself. I gave myself a proper ribbing for that, I can tell you. After all, it was pretty idiotic.

That was an instinctive reaction, but if you pick it apart you can see why it's effective. For one thing, being amused by my own idiocy stopped me being stressed about being covered in cold coffee. It stopped me taking myself too seriously. For another thing, it's much healthier to tease myself for being daft than to denigrate myself seriously for making a stupid mistake.

Your inner dialogue is important – it happens for a lot of your day, and if you're always putting yourself down that gets into your psyche, and it can damage your self-esteem. So it's much better to comment on your own behaviour with a bit of gentle mockery. Of course there are different ways to laugh at yourself so please don't do it in a way that makes you feel small and pathetic. The idea is to laugh at yourself with affection. If you do it right, it can be especially helpful for people who find it really hard to be laughed at by other people, in demonstrating how teasing can be affectionate and even bonding.

Of course, you don't have to keep this kind of humour to yourself. You can tell self-deprecating stories, and point out your own shortcomings to other people. In this context, you need to be more careful not to be self-demeaning, but simply to share the humour and maybe bond over similar experiences.

I worked with someone recently who was very overweight and always joking about it, in a way that seemed to reinforce it. She seemed embarrassed about it and instinctively wanted to get the jokes in before anyone else did. However no one else wanted to make fun of her. She was a lovely, warm person and her weight wasn't an issue for anyone else. That kind of self-deprecating humour isn't healthy – it was just reinforcing her own negative view of herself. So don't fall into this trap, and be aware of who you're talking to and what you're sending yourself up for.

The biggest benefit I find in making fun of myself is that in order to do it I have to stand back and look at myself in the third person, whether I'm laughing privately at spilling the coffee, or recounting a humorous anecdote in which I'm the butt of the joke. The ability to separate yourself from a situation, and view it from a different standpoint, really helps to reduce the stress.

Believe it or not, science is finally catching up and the latest studies do actually show that laughing at yourself makes you feel better, more optimistic and more resilient when bad things happen (such as throwing coffee over yourself). So if you don't often do this, try it. And if you already do it, do it more. Not only does it strengthen your character so you can pursue success, it also helps you cope way better with all those little day-to-day failures along the way.

> # LAUGHING AT YOURSELF MAKES YOU FEEL BETTER, MORE OPTIMISTIC AND MORE RESILIENT

Accept help

We all go through phases when we have more to cope with than we planned. Maybe there's a massive rush on at work, or family problems at home, or some crisis hits – you're laid up for a couple of weeks, the car breaks down, your house gets burgled, someone is threatening to sue you.* Whatever the problem, you're going to get through it far more easily if you get a bit of help. You'll be back on track much sooner. But only if you say 'yes please' to the offers of help from friends and colleagues.

One of the things I've watched over the years is how some people accept help much more readily than others, and those that do can weather those inevitable storms much more successfully. For your own health, and your ability to progress through life as easily as possible, it's a vital skill to learn. And it is a skill, that comes more naturally to some than others.

I get that some people find this hard, often due to past experiences or influences. Some feel ashamed to ask for help as if it's some kind of weakness. Others don't want to be a burden, or feel they don't need – or even deserve – to be helped. There are people who won't ask for certain kinds of help because they struggle to trust anyone. There are those who don't like to accept favours because they feel it puts them in someone else's debt. All these are understandable feelings, but they're not doing you any good. They're a barrier to getting what you need in order to thrive, especially when times are tough.

Look, you're a Rules Player so there must be times when you see someone else struggling and you offer to help. Would you offer if you thought they didn't deserve or need it? When they say yes, does that make you think they're weak? Or make you think you've got leverage over them? Of course not. So if you find this hard, try to see things from that perspective. If your best friend was in the

---

* It's OK, I know it's unjustified – because you're a Rules Player

same position, would you be advising them not to take help from anyone? No you wouldn't. So when you offer help to someone who accepts it – watch and learn. You need to develop their skill in saying yes.

I'll tell you something else too, which you might recognise in yourself. People like helping. Yes they do. It gives them a warm feeling, quite rightly. They want to be good and kind and supportive and you're helping them to do that. And it creates a positive bond between the two of you. And while there should be no sense of debt, or 'owing' favours – if help is offered freely it should be treated as free – nevertheless it's much easier to ask for help from someone where you know it will be mutually reciprocated. Personally I find it easier to ask favours of people I know will ask me in future if they need something, than from people who never ask for anything so I won't get the opportunity to help in return. So by accepting help, you are in effect saying 'let me know if I can do anything for you'.

All of which boils down to saying that when you accept help you are actually giving back simply by saying yes – you're giving the other person a warm sense, a strengthened bond of friendship, and someone they can comfortably come to next time they need a bit of practical support.

> ## SO WHEN YOU OFFER HELP TO SOMEONE WHO ACCEPTS IT – WATCH AND LEARN

STUFF

Some people seem to live in neat and tidy houses where everything has a place, and someone has actually bothered to put it there. Some of us live among clutter and confusion, and wouldn't know where to put a thing away even if we wanted to.

The truth is that there is a whole spectrum of obsessively tidy through to impossibly cluttered, and no right and wrong about where you sit on the scale. Except . . . if you get too far towards either end of the spectrum, it can become a problem for you. It takes over.

It's true for most of us that internal – emotional and mental – order is easier to achieve if our external spaces are in order. I came to realise that while I can happily live with a certain level of mess, actually I do prefer things not to get too cluttered. Mostly I wasn't addressing it because I wasn't sure how to, and it wasn't that bad, and it wasn't causing me too much trouble. But having learnt to be a bit tidier I have shifted along the spectrum, and I do feel better for it. My head is clearer and I less often feel stressed. And that has positive knock-on effects right across my life. As you'll see, scientific studies show that my experience isn't unusual, and reducing clutter is shown to have psychological benefits.

If your surroundings get out of your control, it interferes with your sense of control over the rest of your life – and that's the thing I want you to feel on top of in order to be successful. So the Rules in this section are all about making sure that the property and possessions you live and work among aren't getting in your way emotionally (as well as physically).

Order beats chaos

If you're fairly messy, and your house or apartment is pretty cluttered, that's OK. It's not a sin. There's a school of thought which says that it's morally better to be tidy, and you 'shouldn't' be messy. I don't subscribe to that. It's entirely up to you how you live and other people don't have to like it. You might not like their painfully tidy take-your-shoes-off-before-you-come-in houses, though you're too polite to say so.

Right, that's our starting point. You can be as messy as you like in your own home. However, I'd like to persuade you that it would benefit you – it's not about anyone else's opinion – if you could learn to be a bit tidier. Being tidy is a skill (which doesn't come naturally to me) but it's still one worth learning. Like riding a bicycle or cooking pasta or using a spreadsheet. And like all those skills, you probably don't bother learning them until you see how they will help you. So let's see if I can persuade you that this one is worth learning too.

This book is about smoothing the path to success in whatever areas of life you wish. You want to be able to focus on the big things, the things that matter. And you will, as soon as you've remembered where you put your phone . . . and found your keys . . . that's better. Now you can sit down with a nice cup of coffee and get planning. Oh, hang on, there doesn't seem to be any milk . . .

Listen, on the most basic level, being messy just makes it harder to find things, to keep track of things. Everything takes longer when you have to hunt for your keys before you go out, or spend ages looking for that letter from the insurance people, or for a clean pair of trousers you can wear. It might seem like normal life to you, but think about how much time and headspace it occupies. Imagine if all those things were simple because you could put your hands on them all instantly, or the laundry was up-to-date, or you never ran out of milk. Not to mention those intermittent minor crises that are far more disruptive, like locking yourself out of the house, or realising only when the car breaks down that you forgot to renew your AA or RAC membership.

But that's only half the story – all that wasted time, low-level stress, disruption. Because there's also what goes on inside your head. It's really hard to focus on anything important when you can't find your phone, or you're fretting about what you can wear that's clean. This isn't just my personal experience, having learnt to be more organised than I used to be. There's a solid body of research that backs it up, showing that people who live in more cluttered spaces typically have higher levels of stress and irritability, and are less productive and less able to focus. Whereas an uncluttered home makes everyone feel calmer, and gives children a greater sense of security and stability too. This isn't about those people who have a significant problem with hoarding and can barely get in through their front doors. This research is about everyday, you-and-me levels of mess.

If you want to be a clear thinker who can sail through life success-fully, you need your mind to be organised and streamlined so you can focus, think straight, be productive and feel calm.

I'm well aware that being unorganised is just normal for some people, but there are plenty of strategies that anyone can use which mean it's not inevitable. Even the messiest of us have the capability to learn to be tidier and more streamlined. All you have to do is recognise the need for it, and the Rules in this section will show you that you can do it.

AN UNCLUTTERED HOME MAKES EVERYONE FEEL CALMER

Chill

I hope Rule 91 has reassured you, if you're naturally messy, that it's not wrong. It's just unhelpful to you. What might seem more surprising is that the same is true of the people right at the other end of the spectrum. It's unhelpful to be excessively tidy and organised too.* Again, there are no moral judgements around any of this. Being tidy isn't virtuous or superior. It's simply more efficient – until it goes too far.

The object of the exercise here isn't to have a tidy house or a neat desk. The aim is for you to be in charge of your life, and not to be controlled by the state of your living or working environment. Just as a messy apartment makes it harder for you to get through your day easily and concentrate on the things that are important, so does a house or an office that *has* to be impeccably tidy at all times.

There are those among us** who feel compelled to clear up after every meal before they can sit down, even when there's a reason not to – it might mean missing the start of a favourite programme, or arriving late to an appointment, or not having enough time to call a friend who's unwell. Yes, in the interests of not being messy it's more efficient to clear up straight after a meal, but you have to be able to let it go just occasionally when there's a good reason. Otherwise your drive to be tidy is controlling you, and I want you to be the one in charge.

I do have a bit of a gripe about the way the term OCD gets bandied about. People will say they're a bit OCD about a certain thing when they just mean they're a bit picky. OCD is a serious condition – and not one I'm qualified to address here (or anywhere else). However it is a spectrum, and some people operate at the less debilitating end of it. It might be that you have a predisposition

---

*   I really hope my wife doesn't catch me saying that
** Some of us may even be married to one of them

that hasn't been triggered, or a very mild form of OCD, or you may have some other reason entirely for feeling driven to create order in your life even when it serves no useful purpose, or even hinders you.

This is about control. It's important that you don't allow being tidy and organised to overrule everything else. If you – and people around you – can't relax in case a drink gets spilt, or a document hasn't been filed by lunchtime, or a kitchen spoon gets put away in the wrong drawer, your path through life is made rougher, not smoother. So recognise if this is one of your traits, and understand this: you might feel more in control if everything is in its place, but you're actually less in control if you don't have a choice about doing it.

Lighten up! Chill! Listen to your friends and family dropping hints that you need to relax. If you really can't do this, and think you may have a disorder of some kind, please ignore me and consider asking for professional help. However if you are psychologically capable of loosening up a bit, it's wise to do it now – before the habit becomes more ingrained. You can still live in a tidy and organised world, but don't lose that ability to be flexible when it makes more sense.

> ## YOUR DRIVE TO BE TIDY IS CONTROLLING YOU, AND I WANT YOU TO BE THE ONE IN CHARGE

RULE 93

Analyse yourself

It's helpful to understand why you live in an unorganised or cluttered way. Self-awareness and all that – it's always useful to get to the bottom of these things. There are lots of strategies that will help you clear your physical space, and your headspace, and knowing the underlying reason for the mess can help you pick out the most appropriate ones for you.

Some people grow up surrounded by clutter. I know families where every room in the house is full of junk, there are no clear surfaces anywhere in the kitchen or bathroom, there's laundry everywhere in various stages of being cleaned, and half the cupboards won't close. Nothing ever gets thrown out and clothes the teenage kids wore when they were five are still lying around in boxes. Some people who grow up in this kind of household just regard it as normal and continue to live the same way without questioning it.

There's also a sizeable category of people who live surrounded by mess because they don't know how not to. They haven't worked out how to address it, so they've learnt to live with it. Maybe it's not really their ideal scenario, but it's the only one they know. If you fall into this group, the next few Rules are going to answer some of those questions for you.

I know quite a few people who simply don't care enough about being tidy to bother. They're not sufficiently interested to make the effort. I hope – if this is you – that I've convinced you it is worth the effort. I would add that some people in this category end up living with tidy people and do start to make at least some effort, if only out of consideration for their flatmate or partner, and generally discover (if they're honest with themselves) that they benefit too.

There are also people who struggle to be organised due to some kind of condition, such as ADHD or autism, which may or may not have been diagnosed. Of course not everyone with this kind of condition finds organisation hard, but some certainly do. The good news is that there are plenty of hacks which can make a huge difference. It's not unusual for some of these people to go through childhood and the teenage years surrounded by chaos, bedrooms so deep in mess and clothes they can't remember what colour the carpet is, but then become perfectly tidy and organised once they get into their late teens or early twenties and work out how it's done.

You might tell yourself (as I did) that you like being a messy person. You're wild and free and spontaneous and devil-may-care, and organising your spice rack in alphabetical order just doesn't suit the vibe. But this is simply an excuse for not being better organised, perhaps coupled with a lack of understanding of why you would want to be – which should now be clear.

And look, nobody needs to arrange their spice rack alphabetically.[*] The aim is not to win prizes for neatness, or develop the world's most perfect filing system, or colour code your laundry. You're just trying to get to a point where your headspace isn't cluttered by trying to function surrounded by mess, and to stop wasting time and focus on looking for everyday items you've lost yet again, or being interrupted by emergencies that should have been dealt with routinely days or weeks ago. That's all. You don't need perfection. Any improvement is worth having, and once you've seen the value of it, you'll be motivated to keep improving until you reach the point where it's all running smoothly and you feel calmer, and more able to focus. That, by definition, is good enough.

> # THE AIM IS NOT TO WIN PRIZES FOR NEATNESS

[*] Apart from my wife, apparently

RULE 94

Just start

I'm thinking you may now be sitting in your house, or maybe at your desk, amid a fair degree of mess and clutter and perhaps feeling that maybe you should be doing something about it, but what, and how? Don't panic, this is all achievable, and we'll be looking at some of the specifics in the next few pages.

Meantime, where you do begin? Listen, this isn't going to work unless you believe it will, because you'll be half-hearted about it and then abandon it when it isn't falling into place effortlessly. So what you need to do is get some real wins fast, even if it's not the whole picture. That way you'll realise that you can do this, and you'll be inspired to extend those smaller achievements across the other areas you need to.

My advice would be to pick a room in your house that needs addressing, but isn't overly complicated. Maybe the bathroom or the bedroom might be good places to start. They're usually more self-contained than the kitchen or living room, which often turn out to be full of things that belong in other rooms, or you aren't sure what to do with. By comparison the bathroom and bedroom usually contain things that belong there – but not on the floor – plus things that need throwing out. And maybe one or two other manageable categories, like clothes that need washing.

Pretend the rest of the house isn't there, and don't think about what might need doing in the kitchen or the garage. Just focus on getting this one room straight. It might even be just half a room, it might be the car or the garden shed or the desk. Whatever you feel you can face and make a significant difference to.

Now. The important thing is not to backslide, so once you've tidied this room (well done, by the way) it's more important to keep it clear than to move on to the next room before you're ready. If you move to the kitchen and within days the bedroom is a mess again, you'll start wondering what the point is. Whereas if in a week or two the bedroom still looks good, you'll be wanting to get the same effect across the whole apartment or house.

You'll need to judge this one for yourself. If you're confident that now one room is straight, keeping it that way will be a doddle, then go ahead and crack on with the next room (or shed, desk, whatever). However, if you're not sure you can trust yourself to keep on top of it, it would be better to focus on this one space until you've proved to yourself you can do it. Then when you move on you'll do it confidently, knowing it's just a matter of time before you've worked through the whole apartment.

So to begin with, you're looking for small but sustainable successes. Once you realise you can do this, that's the time to put your foot on the gas a bit. It doesn't matter if it takes a few weeks to work through the place – you might only have time at weekends, or the odd burst in the evenings – but if it takes too long you risk grinding to a halt before you've made the improvements you need to.

> WHAT YOU NEED TO DO IS
> GET SOME REAL WINS FAST

There's a place for everything

Now, before we start, there's one more thing I need to talk to you about. Losing things – phones, keys, wallet. Is this you? If so, you need this Rule. I know someone with a diagnosed condition that is often associated with these kinds of short-term memory and distraction difficulties. So he has every excuse for mislaying things routinely. However, he never loses anything important. Why not? Because for him the problems were so great that he developed near-foolproof strategies to prevent it happening. And if he can do it, so can you.

I've talked to him about this and indeed adopted some of his ideas. They're based on habit. It can take a week or two to get into a new habit but, once it's established, habit is a powerful tool so harness it. Once you've established a routine, your unconscious mind will stick to it even when you aren't consciously thinking about it, or you become distracted.

The essential Rule is that there should be only one place where a thing lives. Keys – on a table just inside the front door, or in a bowl in the kitchen. Doesn't matter where, just pick a sensible spot. Ditto for your phone, your wallet, the dog's lead, your toothbrush, whatever it is you tend to lose. Just the one place where it lives, and you never put it down anywhere else.

Now you put those two things together – spend a few days really focusing on your habit of putting the keys here, the phone there, maybe with help if you can from a partner or housemate. The second you come into the house, or undress for bed – whatever – it's your first action to put the thing in its allotted place. It will be hardly any time before it would feel really weird to put them anywhere else. Even if you're busy talking on the phone as you come in through the front door, you'll find you've instinctively put your keys in the right place. Bingo!

You'll have to decide whether to introduce this system in one go for all the things you typically mislay, or whether to learn to keep track of your keys first, then progress on to your wallet next. You may also have to modify the system to incorporate things like moving pocket items from one set of pockets to another. You understand the principle now though, so you can adapt it as you need. Just come up with something that can easily become a habit. For example, if you keep things in your coat pocket and only occasionally wear a different coat, make it a habit to remove things from the pockets *every* time you take the coat off. That way you reinforce it every time, and it doesn't matter which coat you put on tomorrow.

If losing things is a big problem for you, this is going to save you a lot of time and stress. Imagine how lovely it will be never to have to search for anything before you go out. So you might want to get this sorted before you graduate to clearing the rest of the clutter and muddle around you.

HABIT IS A POWERFUL TOOL
SO HARNESS IT

Decide what to keep, not what to throw

There are two kinds of clearing you can do, broadly. One of those is getting a messy jumbly room or desk where you can't find anything into a state of order – at least sufficient order to be able to find things and to function with a clear head. And then there's the big clear-out you might need because you need to redecorate and can't currently get inside the door, or it's time to address the sacks of kids toys they outgrew years ago, or your dad is coming to live with you and you need to clear out the box room for him. Even the tidiest people occasionally have to do this.

I'm going to start with this type of clearing, because if the place is really cluttered it needs to be done before you can think about the day-to-day sorting out. A lot of the same approaches apply to both, but the additional factor in a major clear-out is that a lot of stuff needs to be got rid of entirely. So this Rule is about getting rid of stuff, rather than just putting it away where it belongs.

In some ways this is the easier version of de-cluttering because you can throw out loads of things without having to think much about each one individually. When a whole cupboard, room, house needs to be cleared out, you're sorting everything into broad categories. At its simplest there are two 'piles' items can go into: keep, or bin. For most people however the 'bin' pile will be subdivided into something like: charity shop, recycling, bin. Plus maybe a pile of baby things to pass on to your sister, for example.

If you're moving house, I would absolutely urge you to go through this process alongside the packing up, or just before. You don't want to go through the effort and expense of moving things you won't need, and just think how good it will feel to move into the new place with only the stuff you actually want, and no extra clutter. Not to mention how much faster that will make the process of moving in and getting settled.

Once you get into the swing of this, most people find it pretty cathartic. Just open up the cupboard, or wade into the room, and as you pick up each item, put it into the appropriate pile. If the 'keep' pile ends up way smaller than what you started with, you're achieving what you need to. You didn't need my help for that. But what if the 'keep' pile is still looking much too big? It can be hard to throw things out.

The key here is not to look at a pile of clothes or a record collection or a bookshelf and ask yourself what you can get rid of. You need to assume you're getting rid of it all and then allow yourself to pick out a few things to keep. How many depends on circumstances – one wardrobe's worth of clothes maybe, or one box of records. You may find this challenging but I promise it gets easier with practice, especially as you see the space starting to clear and can get excited about how it will be once you've finished. Maybe promise yourself a revamp of the room once it's done. If you really struggle to get rid of things, and have the space, you can put things in bags or boxes and store them in a garage or attic for six months. If you haven't missed the contents in that time, then chuck them out (without going through them wistfully first). This can work well with kids' toys – if they don't notice it's gone, you can safely take it to the charity shop.

Keep moving things on so you can see the place clearing before your eyes – fill up boxes or bags and then take them to the tip or the charity shop, start listing items to sell on online marketplaces, get down to the next car boot sale, stack the boxes for moving house in another room. You'll really see the progress you're making.

> # I PROMISE IT GETS EASIER
> # WITH PRACTICE

RULE 97

Make things tidy

So you're standing in the middle of the room, surrounded by stuff – on the floor, the surfaces, maybe even pushing its way out of cupboards and drawers. Ummm . . . where to start? For a lot of people this is exactly the problem. It's not that you don't want the room to be neater, you just have no idea how you're supposed to make it happen. Well don't fret. There's a way to do this that is surprisingly easy.

The starting point is to take one category of items and just deal with those. For example it might be clothes all over the floor, or if it's a child's room it might be Lego,[*] or on a desk it might be paid bills, or empty coffee mugs. You really want an easy win at this stage so here are some pointers to help you choose:

- Pick something that will make a noticeable difference as fast as possible, so probably something you can see from the door rather than the inside of a cupboard (unless the cupboard is your whole focus for today)

- Choose an item you know what to do with – put it in the laundry or the cupboard or the toy box, for example

- Have somewhere to put rubbish right from the start – whether that's worn-out underwear or empty envelopes, you'll start using it early on

While you're collecting up the clothes or Lego or dirty coffee cups, you want to be reasonably blinkered. Don't worry about everything else – just focus on the thing you're clearing. When you're done, you should be able to stand back and feel really positive about the improvement you've made.

Now move on to the next thing, and again choose the most straightforward thing you can. I know that in the back of your

---

[*] In which case you definitely want to start with that, before you tread on it

mind you're worrying about how you'll cope with some of the other stuff when you get that far but listen, leave that until last and by the time you get to it the room will be almost clear and you'll have done so well you'll feel ready to tackle anything.

There's an alternative to the categories approach – it's the same thing but with physical spaces. So first you deal with the desk, then the floor, then the pile of stuff on the chair, or whatever. You can alternate – clear the clothes, then deal with the shelf behind the basin, then the out-of-date meds around the room – as you wish. However if there are obvious big categories like clothes strewn everywhere, clearing them will probably give you the biggest boost so they might be best to do first.

Now here's the most important category you've been fretting about – things you actually don't know what to do with. Don't keep picking them up, feeling hopeless, shrugging and putting them down again. That won't help. Have somewhere for them to belong – a pile for 'things you don't know what to do with'. Put them there, leave them for now, and get on with all the things you *can* sort out. Not only does that make your life easier, but it has a useful purpose too. Once everything else is done, and you come back to this pile, you should find it's big enough to contain categories of its own. You'll look at it and think, 'Ah – I need a space for spare flowerpots' or 'Let me find a box and all the kids' loose arts and crafts things can go in there'.

Before you know it, the room, desk, shed, cupboard, is sorted, or near enough. The last few uncategorisable items, that can't be disposed of, should be easy to find places for now.

> # YOU'LL HAVE DONE SO WELL YOU'LL FEEL READY TO TACKLE ANYTHING

Keep things tidy

It's one thing to have a blitz and tidy up your cupboard, your room, your flat. It's another thing to keep it that way so you don't have to repeat the exercise every few months. That's what we want to achieve – space to live and work that is always effortlessly clear so you have room to think and room to function effectively. And that's what this Rule is all about.

Broadly speaking, the trick to this lies in countless tiny acts of tidying and clearing every day, which are so small as to be barely noticeable. So they're no hardship, and before long they become second nature. You don't even notice you're picking up your empty cup when you're heading to the kitchen, or dropping your clothes in the laundry basket when you take them off, because it's instinctive. Once again, habit is your friend.

The first thing to do is to identify where you need these strategies. Often you can usefully do this while you're clearing. You'll realise that if you kept the laundry basket in the bathroom instead of the bedroom you'd be more likely to use it, or that if the kids had a cupboard specifically for their art stuff it would be easier to clear away. It's not just about everything having a place, it's about everything having a usable and effective place. What are the things that most often get left lying around? They're the ones that need a designated place. If they already have one, it's obviously not working, so change it.

Here's another habit you need to get into: any time you find yourself unsure where to put something, have a rule that you don't just dump it to sort out later. That won't happen, will it? So work out where it goes. If you're in a mad rush and simply can't deal with it now, dump it somewhere so inconvenient you can't forget about it. In the kitchen sink, or blocking the TV screen or something. Then deal with it properly once you have five minutes (don't just move it again).

You should find that once your place is tidy you're motivated to keep it that way, so none of this should be too onerous. However you don't want to be rushing up and downstairs all day with items that belong in the bathroom, the kitchen, the living room, the bedroom. So it can help to have a spot allocated for things you're going to take with you next time you go upstairs, or into the kids' bedroom or wherever. For example, anything to go upstairs can live on the bottom step until you're next going that way. Next time, mind you – don't leave things piling up there for days or you've just moved your previous clutter problem to a different part of the house.

You can have a spot in your bathroom for things that need to go downstairs (packaging to recycle?), and a place inside the front door for anything you need to take with you when you next go out – post, or meetings files, or your friend's birthday gift for when you meet up tomorrow.

Unless you live alone, this will all be much easier if everyone is on board. So encourage your partner or housemates to join in – at least in communal areas. Children especially need to learn to do this – you'll be giving them a huge gift for the future if you can teach them how to live without clutter and mess. When mine were smaller, they each had their own step at the bottom of the stairs, and were encouraged* to take their pile of stuff up to their room every day.

> # YOU SHOULD FIND THAT ONCE YOUR PLACE IS TIDY YOU'RE MOTIVATED TO KEEP IT THAT WAY

---

* That's my word for it, and I'm sticking to it

Resist expansion

Now here's something it took me a while to learn, but it's an invaluable way of keeping the amount of stuff I own to a minimum. It used to be bookshelves. I'd keep acquiring books – I love browsing a second hand bookshop if only to drink in the smell, but I always come away with something too. The books kept piling up. Eventually, fed up with all the piles of books that didn't fit on the shelves, I'd think of somewhere to put another bookcase or fit a couple more shelves. I barely noticed how much of my living space they occupied (after all books are lovely things to share space with). But not only were they taking up space, it was also space that I could have used for something else that now had nowhere to live.

Eventually I had to do a big sort out in order to decorate or something, and I realised how many of these books I simply didn't need. Especially in this age of the internet, I don't want a travel guide from 10 years ago next time I go to Paris – I'll just look up where to stay or what to visit online, where prices and opening hours will be up-to-date. The same goes for reference books. Who uses a thesaurus these days when there are so many available online? Then there were all the novels I'd read once but wasn't going to read again . . . it started to dawn on me that I simply didn't need most of these books. I could give them away or donate them and free up loads of space.

So I sorted through the books, and kept only the ones I was actually going to look at, plus a few that had sentimental value. After decorating, I put back enough shelving for the books I'd kept, plus a bit of room for expansion, and then dispensed with the rest of the shelves. It was hugely cathartic and cleared masses of space, and I've never regretted it. More importantly, I've never added any more shelving. My rule now is that if I run out of shelf space for books, I go through the ones I have and get rid of everything I'm not going to look at again.

And – in case you're not a bookaholic and can't see how this Rule would apply to you – I haven't stopped at bookshelves. I work mostly from home, and in my study I have a two-drawer filing cabinet. When this started to overflow I was busy wondering how I could fit in another filing cabinet, when it occurred to me that maybe filing cabinets were like bookshelves. Yep! Turns out that so long as I clear out the old and out-of-date paperwork, I only need two drawers. So that's the rule. If you can't fit everything in don't expand, just clear out the dead wood.

You know what? Lots of things turn out to be like bookshelves. Wardrobes are an excellent example. I remember helping a friend sort through clothes when they were moving house. Their wall-to-wall wardrobe had slowly expanded and taken over the spare bedroom one too, as well as a new cupboard they'd had to install specially on the landing. After clearing out ahead of their move, they only kept enough clothes to fill half their original wardrobe. If they'd kept on top of things, they'd never have needed to clutter their landing, and they could have used the spare bedroom cupboards for something else.

Kitchen food cupboards (just remove everything out of date or unused in the last year), or shelves of baking equipment, boxes and cupboards of hobby-related stuff in the garage or box room, kids' toy chests, the list goes on. Just have a Rule that you don't expand, you clear back to the level of stuff that will fit. You'd be surprised how easy it is to do once you focus your mind on reducing rather than expanding.

> # IF YOU CAN'T FIT EVERYTHING IN DON'T EXPAND, JUST CLEAR OUT THE DEAD WOOD

Think before you buy

One of my brothers has three questions he always asks before buying anything:

1. Do I need it?

2. Can I afford it?

3. Do I have somewhere to put it?

For the purposes of this group of Rules it's the third question that I'm interested in, although I wouldn't argue with the second one either. (The first question is helpful, but if every purchase was based on need alone, we'd never buy anything just because it was beautiful or made us happy.) This Rule also applies to acquiring things that other people are throwing out, or that you've found in a skip. Anything you could say no to if you chose. The less you have in the first place, the simpler your life will be.

Look, if you're serious about living in a clearer, more streamlined environment, you'll make it so much easier for yourself if you don't accumulate stuff in the first place. You don't have to become a minimalist, all smooth shiny surfaces and not a door handle in sight. It's fine to have pictures on the walls and a throw over the sofa. Even a small collection of current books and magazines on the coffee table – although it's good to have room to fit the odd coffee mug on it too. But the less you have, the less you have to tidy away, and the more space you have to store it.

So think about your buying (or acquiring) habits. Notice as you clear up what are the things you most typically buy and then never use – clothes? exotic cooking ingredients? books? stationery? spare car parts? scented candles? Those are the things to question next time. When and how do you buy them, and how can you stop yourself doing it mindlessly?

When I was young, if you wanted to buy clothes – even underwear – you had to get up and dressed and get yourself on the bus to the shops, and then traipse round looking for the right thing. Nowadays you don't even have to get out of bed. You can just go online. In many ways it's a fantastic example of the wonder of modern technology, but it doesn't half make it easy to click a button and buy a thing without really thinking. And how often do we get that lovely dopamine hit from buying something and then the novelty wears off, sometimes even before it's been delivered.

So work out what ground rules will slow you down and stop you acquiring things you don't really want or need. For a start, you can work out where a thing will live before you allow yourself to buy it. If you over-purchase in a particular category – clothes, for example – maybe ban yourself from buying online. If you have to muster the time and effort to go to real shops, that will reduce your opportunities to buy. For items above a certain value, make yourself take a cooling off period of one or two days before you go back and buy. Or only shop with someone you know will talk you down if necessary. Or cash only and no credit card.

Above all, recognise that if you only buy the things you need and have room for, you'll not only save money but you'll make it so much easier to maintain the streamlined, clutter-free, effortless lifestyle that leaves you free to succeed where it really matters to you. Your focus will improve, you'll be more productive, and your sense of calm and well-being will increase. If that's not a recipe for success, I don't know what is.

> # THE LESS YOU HAVE IN THE FIRST PLACE, THE SIMPLER YOUR LIFE WILL BE

Create your own Rules

Remember, I'm not the only one who can observe other people and see what works for them that could work for me too. So keep a look out for new Rules, and when you identify one I haven't included here, note it down. Keep a list of additional Rules you want to emulate and write them down. You can share them too so we all benefit.

If you're wondering what makes a good Rule, it's a guiding principle that works in (almost) all cases for people of all kinds. It's not just a handy trick or a useful tip (e.g. use coloured stickers to organise yourself, or keep your car de-icer in the house and not the car – you always need it when you're at home anyway, and that way the bottle isn't freezing cold – or never eat anything bigger than your head). Useful as these pointers are, they're not Rules in the sense I use the word. A good Rule is about changing your attitude or shifting your mindset so you approach problems or situations from a different perspective.

It seems a shame to keep these new Rules to yourself, so please feel free to share them with other people. If you'd like to share them on my Facebook page I'd love to hear from you at www.facebook.com/richardtemplar. Either post a single Rule, or maybe put together your top five and post them so other readers can get the benefit.

When you decide to share a Rule, it's a good idea to explain it, and then to give an example or two so other people can see how it works in practice, to help them understand how to apply it to their own lives.

A Rule is a Rule, it doesn't matter whether it's me or you or anyone else who has noted it down (in fact, it doesn't matter if no one has identified it yet, it's still a Rule). If it works, not only for you but for other people too, it's worth sharing. So please post your new Rules and, who knows, I may even assemble the best of them together sometime in the future.

These are the Rules

I have spent a lifetime watching, learning and distilling the Rules of how happy and successful people behave. I have observed what it is that these people do, and others do not. Whether it's at work or in their relationships, as parents or managing their money, I can tell you why their lives run more smoothly than other people's.

The Rules aren't orders. You don't *have* to obey them. I'm not telling you how you should live your life. I'm just passing on what I've learnt myself, in the hope you can make use of it. You'll be happier and more successful if you follow the Rules, but it's your call.

Some of these Rules – many of them – are common sense. They're a reminder, not a revelation. But somehow you need to see them in black and white to realise that you've wandered off the track. Others may take a bit longer to get your head round. And you might even disagree with a few. That's fine – you're allowed to think for yourself. In fact, it's actively encouraged.

There are several books in the Rules series, to help you make a success of just about every part of your life:

The Rules of Work
The Rules of Life
The Rules of Management
The Rules of Wealth
The Rules of Parenting
The Rules of Love
The Rules to Break
The Rules of People
The Rules of Thinking
The Rules of Living Well
The Rules of Everything

Just to give you a sample, the next couple of pages are a 'one Rule' taster of *The Rules of Wealth*.

Richard Templar

Anybody can be wealthy – you just need to apply yourself

The lovely thing about money is that it really doesn't discriminate. It doesn't care what colour or race you are, what class you are, what your parents did, or even who you *think* you are. Each and every day starts with a clean slate so that no matter what you did yesterday, today begins anew and you have the same rights and opportunities as everyone else to take as much as you want. The only thing that can hold you back is yourself and your own money myths (see Rule 7).

Of the wealth of the world each has as much as they take. What else could make sense? There is no way money can know who is handling it, what their qualifications are, what ambitions they have or what class they belong to. Money has no ears or eyes or senses. It is inert, inanimate, impassive. It hasn't a clue. It is there to be used and spent, saved and invested, fought over, seduced with and worked for. It has no discriminatory apparatus so it can't judge whether you are 'worthy' or not.

I have watched a lot of extremely wealthy people and the one thing they all have in common is that they have nothing in common – apart from all being Rules Players of course. The wealthy are a diverse band of people – the least likely can be loaded. They vary from the genteel to the uncouth, the savvy to the plain stupid, the deserving to the undeserving. But each and every one of them has stepped up and said, 'Yes please, I want some of that'. And the poor are the ones saying, 'No thank you, not for me, I am not worthy. I am not deserving enough. I couldn't. I mustn't. I shouldn't'.

That's what this book is about – challenging your perceptions of money and the wealthy. We all assume the poor are poor because of circumstances, their background, their upbringing, their nurture. But if you have the means to buy a book such as this and live in comparative security and comfort in the world then you too have the power to be wealthy. It may be hard. It may be tough but it is doable. And that is Rule 1 – anyone can be wealthy, you just need to apply yourself. All the other Rules are about that application.

> ## YOU HAVE THE SAME RIGHTS AND OPPORTUNITIES AS EVERYONE ELSE TO TAKE AS MUCH AS YOU WANT